Literacy, Numeracy and Problem Solving in Technology-Rich Environments

FRAMEWORK FOR THE OECD SURVEY OF ADULT SKILLS

OECD

This work is published on the responsibility of the Secretary-General of the OECD. The opinions expressed and arguments employed herein do not necessarily reflect the official views of the Organisation or of the governments of its member countries.

This document and any map included herein are without prejudice to the status of or sovereignty over any territory, to the delimitation of international frontiers and boundaries and to the name of any territory, city or area.

Please cite this publication as:
OECD (2012), *Literacy, Numeracy and Problem Solving in Technology-Rich Environments: Framework for the OECD Survey of Adult Skills*, OECD Publishing.
http://dx.doi.org/10.1787/9789264128859-en

ISBN 978-92-64-12880-4 (print)
ISBN 978-92-64-12885-9 (PDF)

Photo credits:
Getty Images © Tetra Images
Fotolia © ag visuell
iStockphoto © Joshua Hodge Photography
Stocklib © Kheng Ho Toh
Getty Images © Monty Rakusen
Stocklib © Fernando Blanco Calzada

Foreword

The Programme for the International Assessment of Adult Competencies (PIAAC) is an international assessment of adult skills managed by the OECD which is currently being implemented by 25 countries in Europe, the Americas and Asia. PIAAC will provide one of the richest sources of data regarding the foundation skills of adults, the skills that they use in work and other contexts and correlates of skills such as demographic characteristic, family background, education, employment, income and outcomes such as civic participation and health.

Development of assessment frameworks is a central component of the approach to assessment underlying PIAAC. These frameworks provide an agreed definition of what should be measured and the identification of characteristics which can be used in the construction and interpretation of tasks. In other words they define what is meant by "literacy", "numeracy" and "problem solving in technology-rich environments" in PIAAC.

Draft frameworks for each of the assessment domains were developed by dedicated expert groups under the leadership of Stan Jones (literacy), Iddo Gal (numeracy), Jean-François Rouet (problem solving in technology-rich environments). The reading components framework was prepared by John Sabatini and Kelly Bruce.

This document which summarises the work of the expert groups was prepared by William Thorn. Andreas Schleicher, Irwin Kirsch and Claudia Tamassia offered valuable comments during the drafting. Marilyn Achiron, Fionnuala Canning and Elizabeth Del Bourgo provided editorial assistance. Niccolina Clements, Sabrina Leonarduzzi and Elisabeth Villoutreix co-ordinated the production process.

Angel Gurría
OECD Secretary-General

Table of Contents

FIGURES

TABLES

Introduction

WHAT SKILLS ARE BEING MEASURED?

The Programme for the International Assessment of Adult Competencies (PIAAC) is a global assessment of adult skills, managed by the OECD and implemented by 25 countries in Europe, the Americas and Asia. Data are being collected from August 2011 to March 2012 and results will be available at the end of 2013.

This document provides an overview of the skills that are assessed in PIAAC – literacy, numeracy and problem solving in technology-rich environments – with a focus on the key features of the frameworks guiding the development of the assessments, in particular, the definitions of the different assessment domains and the variables that guide selection of assessment tasks.

Developing assessment frameworks is a central component of the approach to assessment underlying PIAAC and its predecessors. The frameworks provide an agreed definition of what should be measured and identify characteristics that can be used in the construction and interpretation of tasks. In other words, they define what is meant by "literacy", "numeracy" and "problem solving in technology-rich environments" in PIAAC.

The frameworks for each of the assessment domains are presented in Sections 4 to 6. A brief summary of the objectives and design of PIAAC, as well as an overview of its relationship to previous international assessments of adult skills, is undertaken in Sections 2 and 3, respectively.

Draft frameworks for each of the assessment domains were developed by dedicated expert groups and have been published separately (PIAAC Literacy Expert Group, 2009; PIAAC Numeracy Expert Group, 2009; PIAAC Problem Solving Expert Group 2009; and Sabatini and Bruce 2009).[1] This document summarises this work. It also includes examples of the items and stimuli used to measure proficiency in the domains covered by the assessment.

Note

1. The membership of the expert groups is presented in Annex A.

References

PIAAC Literacy Expert Group (2009), *PIAAC Literacy: Conceptual Framework*, OECD Education Working Papers No. 34, OECD, Paris. Available on line at: *http://ideas.repec.org/p/oec/eduaab/34-en.html*.

PIAAC Numeracy Expert Group (2009), *PIAAC Numeracy: Conceptual Framework*, OECD Education Working Papers No. 35, OECD, Paris. Available on line at: *http://ideas.repec.org/p/oec/eduaab/35-en.html*.

PIAAC Exert Group in Problem Solving in Technology-Rich Environments (2009), *PIAAC Problem Solving in Technology-rich Environments: Conceptual Framework*, OECD Education Working Papers, No. 36, OECD, Paris. Available on line at: *http://ideas.repec.org/p/oec/eduaab/36-en.html*.

Sabatini, J.P. and **K.M. Bruce** (2009), *PIAAC Reading Components: Conceptual Framework*, OECD Education Working Papers No. 33, OECD, Paris. Available on line at: *http://ideas.repec.org/p/oec/eduaab/33-en.html*.

1

Why Assess the Skills of Adults?

This chapter examines the context in which PIAAC was developed, including fundamental changes in the demand for skills, the liabilities associated with having a low level of skills, particularly in increasingly knowledge-based societies, and the need for comprehensive data on the level and distribution of skills among adults.

The skills that are assessed in PIAAC (literacy, numeracy and problem solving in technology-rich environments) represent cross-cutting cognitive skills that provide a foundation for effective and successful participation in the social and economic life of advanced economies. Understanding the level and distribution of these skills among the adult population in participating countries, as well as the ways such skills are developed and maintained, and the social and economic benefits for individuals, is important for policy makers in a range of areas of social and economic policy.

CHANGING DEMAND FOR SKILLS

Technological change, particularly the increasing presence of information and communication technologies (ICT) in all areas of life, together with changes in the structure of employment has led to a growing demand for higher-level cognitive skills involving the understanding, interpretation, analysis and communication of complex information. Using the categorisation developed by Autor, Levy and Murnane (2003), employment is shifting away from jobs involving routine cognitive and manual tasks and towards jobs involving tasks such as expert thinking (solving problems for which there are no rules-based solutions) and complex communication (interacting with others to acquire or explain information, or persuade others of its implications for action). In the United States, for example, from 1969 to 1999, the demand for tasks requiring expert thinking and complex communication grew rapidly while that for other tasks remained stable or declined sharply, particularly for routine cognitive tasks (Levy and Murnane, 2006, p. 57).

In this context, the adequacy of the supply of these higher-level cognitive skills is a crucial issue for policy. Previous assessments – the International Adults Literacy Survey of 1994-98 (IALS) and the Adult Literacy and Life Skills Survey of 2003-06 (ALL) – showed that large proportions of the adult population in many advanced economies had low levels of proficiency in literacy and numeracy; and ALL provided worrying evidence of stable or declining literacy proficiency across the population as a whole and for individual age groups in a number of countries. As its results will be able to be linked to those from previous international adult skills surveys (see Section 3 below), PIAAC will provide evidence not only on the current level and distribution of skills, but also on the change in literacy and numeracy skills profiles over time. For the first time, PIAAC will offer a measure of problem solving that is directly linked to the ICT-rich environments that characterise jobs with a high information-processing content. Moreover, PIAAC is collecting considerably more information on the use of skills in the workplace than did previous surveys. That, in turn, will facilitate investigation of the effectiveness of matching workers to jobs and of the extent to which the skills possessed by individuals are used in their work.

LOW PROFICIENCY – ITS SCALE AND IMPACT

A basic level of literacy and numeracy is essential for full participation in modern societies. Given the ubiquity of text in all areas of life, individuals must be able to understand and respond appropriately to textual information and communicate in written form in order to fulfil, even minimally, their roles in society, whether as citizen, consumer, parent or employee. The use of numerical tools and models has permeated many jobs, and in many countries individuals are being required to assume more responsibility for matters such as retirement planning. The presence of ICT in the workplace and elsewhere, and related changes in the delivery of many services (e.g. online banking, e-government, electronic shopping), may well have increased the importance of a mastery of basic literacy and numeracy skills in many aspects of modern life.

While there are very few people in most of the advanced countries who could be regarded as illiterate or innumerate, IALS and ALL have both shown that there are, nevertheless, significant numbers of people with poor skills, and that low skill levels are associated with negative outcomes, such as lower wages and greater chances of unemployment and disengagement from the labour market. The results from IALS, in particular, triggered something of a policy shock in many countries, helping to raise awareness of the scale of low literacy proficiency and prompting governments to develop adult literacy and numeracy strategies. In the English-speaking world, for example, IALS inspired the development of adult literacy and numeracy strategies in England, Ireland, New Zealand, Northern Ireland and Scotland.

The scale of low proficiency literacy and numeracy in the adult population remains an issue for policy makers, particularly given the evolution of the labour market and the growing penetration of ICT in all areas of life. PIAAC is considerably expanding the information available regarding persons with low levels of literacy. Such respondents are being directed to a test of component reading skills covering vocabulary knowledge, sentence processing and passage comprehension.

This will considerably increase the base of knowledge regarding low-skilled readers and their level of mastery of the basic building blocks of reading, and will provide some guidance as to appropriate interventions.

Equally important is that a certain level of proficiency in literacy and numeracy appears to be a pre-condition for success in undertaking more complex problem-solving tasks – a skill for which demand appears to be increasing. Results from ALL suggest that individuals with low literacy skills have a very small chance of successfully completing problem-solving tasks.

SKILLS FOR THE INFORMATION AGE

Most of the reading, computational and problem-solving skills relevant to a print environment continue to be relevant in technology-rich environments. However, in these new environments, some aspects of traditional skills assume greater importance. For example, the sheer amount of information, its accessibility and its uncensored nature emphasise the need to be able to connect, evaluate and interpret information. In addition, displays of information in ICT environments have features such as non-linearity, recursiveness and interactivity that do not exist in print-based presentations. The multimodal aspects of computer environments, for example, mean that information is no longer presented in printed texts and graphics but, increasingly, in the form of animation, audio and motion video. In addition, people follow individual pathways when searching for information on the Internet and thus create their own "texts", in the sense that the total set of information that each individual encounters is unique. The skills required to use digital information effectively are less well understood than traditional print skills. Nevertheless, it is clear that it is necessary to expand the concepts of what it means to be literate, numerate and to process information in relation to digital environments.

The assessments of literacy and problem solving in PIAAC have been explicitly developed to reflect the demands of the digital environment. The literacy domain has been defined to cover the skills of reading digital texts in addition to print-based materials, and the assessment includes items using digital texts, such as websites and e-mails as stimuli. The assessment of problem solving has been developed to assess the capacity to find solutions for "information" problems – problems that are defined within a digital environment and necessitate the use of computer applications in order to be solved.

PIAAC will thus provid a more complete picture of the capacity of the adult population to use ICT than has been previously available. In addition to information on the incidence, frequency and type of use of ICT, PIAAC is offering a picture of the proficiency of the adult population using such technologies for defined cognitive goals, such as extracting, interpreting, evaluating and analysing information.

THE OUTPUT AND PERFORMANCE OF EDUCATION SYSTEMS

Good, internationally comparative data regarding performance of school systems as manifested in the proficiency of 15-year-olds in reading, mathematics and science are available from PISA (Programme of International Student Assessment). Assessing adult skills is a way of expanding the understanding how education systems perform by offering a perspective on individuals' outcomes from their "initial" education/training, either in the form of the skills and labour-market status of the age cohort that has recently completed such education/training (e.g. the 25-34 year-old age group), or of individuals who have completed initial education within a defined time period (e.g. within the past five years).

An issue of considerable interest and importance is whether the differences between countries – differences in the observed performances of cohorts of 15-year-olds – are maintained, reduced or increased as the cohorts pass through subsequent education and training. Does the performance of young people in countries that perform relatively poorly in the PISA assessments catch up with that of their peers in better-performing countries or not by the time they have left "initial" education and training? Do the trajectories of achievement growth differ between countries? Are factors such as institutional arrangements (e.g. tracked or comprehensive secondary education) or differing rates of participation in different types of post-secondary education (e.g. vocational education and training, higher education) associated with different patterns of achievement growth?

Direct measures of cognitive skills are seen by some researchers as better indicators of the overall stock of skills (or human capital) in countries than measures of educational attainment, such as highest level of education or years of schooling completed. The main criticism levelled at the use of attainment or years of schooling as an indicator of the

stock of human capital is that it assumes equivalence in the quality of a year of study completed in different eras and in different countries. Some recent studies that have either adjusted years of schooling data for quality, using cognitive test data, or used cognitive test data on its own have found a much stronger link between education and growth than studies using indicators such as years of schooling.[1]

Note

1. Hanushek and Zhang (2006) use data from IALS construct quality-adjusted measures of schooling attained at different time periods and use these along with international literacy test information to estimate returns to skills for 13 countries. Hanushek and Woessmann (2009) use data from international assessments of school students to estimate the impact of education on growth. Coulombe, Tremblay and Marchand (2004) use data from IALS to investigate the relationship between human capital and growth across 14 OECD countries.

References

Autor, D., F. Levy and **R.J. Murnane** (2003), "The Skill Content of Recent Technological Change: An Empirical Exploration", *Quarterly Journal of Economics*, No. 118(4), November, pp. 1279-1334.

Coulombe, S., J.F. Tremblay and **S. Marchand** (2004), *Literacy Scores, Human Capital and Growth across Fourteen OECD Countries*, Statistics Canada, Ottawa.

Hanushek, E.A. and **L. Woessmann** (2009), *Do Better Schools Lead to More Growth? Cognitive Skills, Economic Outcomes, and Causation*, NBER Working Papers No. 14633, National Bureau of Economic Research, Cambridge, Massachusetts.

Hanushek, E. A., and **L. Zhang** (2006), *Quality-Consistent Estimates of International Returns to Skill*, NBER Working Papers No. 12664, National Bureau of Economic Research, Cambridge, Massachusetts.

Levy, F. and **R.J. Murnane** (2006), "Why the Changing American Economy Calls for Twenty-first Century Learning: Answers to Educators' Questions", *New Directions for Youth Development*, No. 110, Summer, pp 53-62.

2

Some Design Features of PIAAC

PIAAC is linked with two international surveys of adult skills: the International Adult Literacy Survey and the Adult Literacy and Life Skills Survey. This chapter describes how PIAAC extends the scope of measurement beyond the skills examined in the other two surveys to include those skills relevant to the digital age, particularly in the domains of literacy and problem solving.

LINKS TO PREVIOUS SURVEYS

Two international surveys of adult skills have been implemented prior to the development of PIAAC – the International Adult Literacy Survey (IALS) of 1994-98 and the Adult Literacy and Life Skills Survey (ALL) of 2003-06.[1] PIAAC considerably extends the scope of the measurement of adult skills to those skills relevant to the digital age, particularly in the domains of literacy and problem solving. At the same time there are links between PIAAC and both ALL and IALS in the domain of literacy and ALL in the domain of numeracy to allow comparison between the results of PIAAC and those of previous assessments. Table 2.1 presents the skill domains assessed in the three assessments. Shading indicates that the assessments in these domains can be linked across surveys.

Table 2.1
Skills Assessed in PIAAC, ALL and IALS

PIAAC (2012)	ALL (2004-2006)	IALS (1994-1998)
Literacy (combined prose and document)	Literacy (combined prose and document*)	Literacy (combined prose and document*)
	Prose literacy	Prose literacy
	Document literacy	Document literacy
Reading components		
Numeracy	Numeracy	
		Quantitative literacy
Problem solving in technology-rich environments		
	Problem solving	

*Rescaled to form a single literacy scale combining the former separate prose and document literacy scales.

The construct of "literacy" has been broadened in PIAAC compared to previous surveys. In particular, it does not distinguish "prose" literacy (the reading of "continuous" texts) from "document" literacy and includes the reading of digital texts as an essential component of reading proficiency in the 21st century. PIAAC will also provide considerably more information regarding the skills of poor readers than has been previously available through the inclusion of an assessment of "reading components". For reporting purposes, data from IALS and ALL is being rescaled onto the new PIAAC literacy scale. In both the domains of literacy and numeracy, approximately 60 percent of items are common to previous PIAAC assessment to ensure comparability.

COMPUTER-BASED ASSESSMENT

PIAAC is delivered as a computer-based assessment. The test application (including the background questionnaire and the direct assessment) is loaded on a laptop computer. The background questionnaire is administered by the interviewer. The majority of respondents complete the assessment on a laptop computer under the supervision of the interviewer. Respondents who have little or no familiarity with computers are directed to a pencil-and-paper version of the assessment that tests skills in the domains of literacy and numeracy only. All respondents, irrespective of whether they take the assessment in the computer or pencil-and-paper format, first take a "core test" to assess their capacity to undertake the full assessment. Those who "fail" the core test are directed to the assessment of reading components. Those who "pass" the core test proceed to the full assessment. Figure 2.1 shows the possible pathways through the assessment.

A feature of the PIAAC assessment is that it includes an adaptive element that makes use of the possibilities provided by automatic scoring. On the basis of their performance at different stages of the assessment, respondents taking the CBA version are directed to different "testlets" that contain items of different average difficulty in the domains of literacy and numeracy.

■ Figure 2.1 ■

PIAAC Main Study Assessment Design

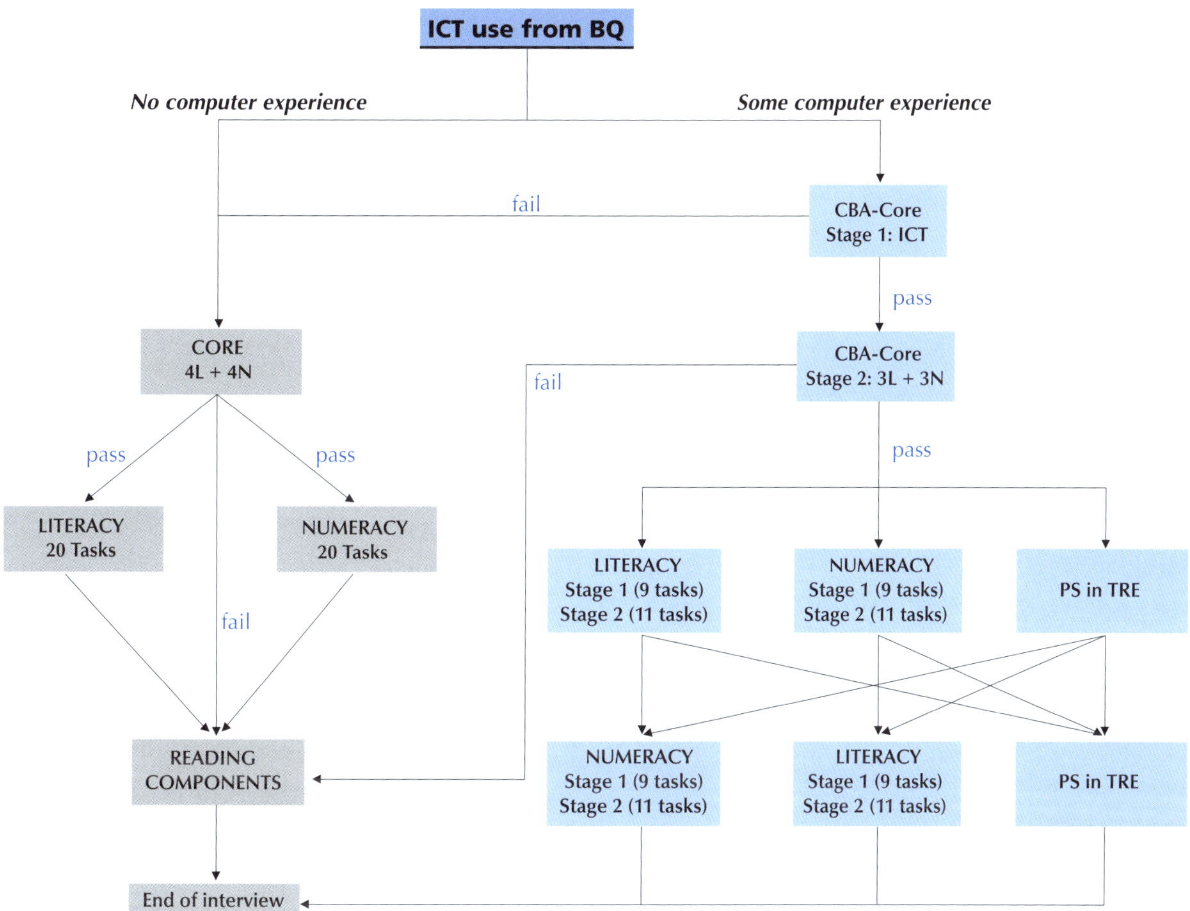

Note

1. See OECD/Statistics Canada (2000, 2005) for information on the methods and results of IALS and ALL, respectively.

References

OECD/Statistics Canada (2000), *Literacy in the Information Age: Final Report of the International Adult Literacy Survey*, OECD Publishing.

OECD/Statistics Canada (2005), Learning a Living: First Results of the Adult Literacy and Life Skills Survey, OECD Publishing.

3

Literacy and Reading Components

This chapter defines PIAAC's concept of literacy as understanding, evaluating, using and engaging with written texts to participate in society, to achieve one's goals, and to develop one's knowledge and potential. It describes the characteristics and aspects of the PIAAC literacy tasks and explores factors affecting task difficulty and the distribution of the test items. Sample items in both literacy and reading components are provided.

DEFINITION OF THE DOMAIN

PIAAC defines literacy as *understanding, evaluating, using and engaging with written texts to participate in society, to achieve one's goals, and to develop one's knowledge and potential.*

The key elements of this definition are developed below.

Written text

PIAAC is an assessment of adults' use and understanding of *written text*. Written text is text (including visual displays, such as graphs) presented in a graphic form accessible in a variety of media (including material printed on paper as well as text displayed on a screen, such as that of a computer, a PDA, an ATM, a BlackBerry® or an iPhone).

Understanding

A basic task for a reader is to construct meaning from a text. This can range from understanding the meaning of individual words to comprehending the underlying theme of a lengthy argument or narrative.

Evaluating

Adult reading involves making judgments about texts. These include questions such as the appropriateness of the text for the task at hand, the credibility of the content and, in some cases, the quality of a text, both as an aesthetic object and as a means of acquiring information. In the case of electronic texts, the issue of their credibility and authenticity is particularly important. Electronic texts can be accessed from a range of sources, the identity and credentials of which are not always clear.

Using

Much adult reading is purposive, i.e. directed towards applying information and ideas in a text to address an immediate task or goal or to reinforce or change beliefs.

Engaging with

Adults differ in how engaged they are with texts and the role reading plays in their lives. Studies have found that engagement with reading (i.e. attitudes towards reading and reading practices) is closely correlated with proficiency.

Participate in society, achieve one's goals, and develop one's knowledge and potential

Reading plays an important role in participating in society, in fulfilling personal aspirations and in continuing learning. It provides the foundation for full and active engagement in many aspects of social life. For example, literacy skills are essential at work and for effectively negotiating complex bureaucracies, accessing services and making informed political decisions.

CATEGORISING TEXTS (TASK CHARACTERISTICS)

The following variables have been used to categorise texts for the purposes of the PIAAC assessment:

- medium (print and digital)
- format (continuous and non-continuous)
- type (rhetorical stance)
- physical layout (type of matrix organisation)
- features unique to digital texts
- social context

Medium

Texts are distinguished in PIAAC as either digital (or electronic) texts or print texts.[1] In some cases, digital texts may be simply copies of printed texts. However, digital texts are distinguished not only by the medium in which they are disseminated but also by the use they make of the text navigation and display features unique to digital devices. A text that can be reproduced in print exactly as it appears on a screen is considered to be a *print* text. A text that cannot be reproduced in print with all of its features intact is considered a *digital* text.[2]

Format

In the literacy frameworks of IALS, ALL and PISA, texts are classified as either continuous (prose) or non-continuous (document) texts. As many texts encountered in real life contain both continuous and non-continuous elements, texts are classified in the following way in PIAAC:

- *Continuous texts*. Normally, this type of text is made up of sentences formed into paragraphs. Examples of continuous texts include newspaper and magazine articles, brochures, manuals, e-mails and many web pages.

- *Non-continuous texts*. This type of text uses explicit typographic features, rather than paragraphs, to organise information in some kind of matrix arrangement. Tables, graphs, charts and forms are all examples of non-continuous texts.

- *Mixed texts*. This type of text has both continuous and non-continuous elements. Examples of mixed texts include web pages with a list of links, newspaper articles that contain graphs or pie charts, and brochures with attached order forms.[3]

- *Multiple texts*. Multiple texts consist of texts that have been generated and that make sense independently of each other. The texts are juxtaposed or loosely linked for a particular purpose.

Text type (rhetorical stance of the text)

Text types (rhetorical stances) constitute ways of organising continuous texts in terms of their content and the purpose of the author. The six types[4] of rhetorical stances identified for PIAAC are as follows:

- *Description* is the type of text in which the information refers to properties of objects *in space*. A page in a manual that identifies the parts of a device such as a washing machine is a description, as is a verbal explanation or depiction of a piece of art.

- *Narration* is the type of text in which the information refers to properties of objects *in time*. Accounts of a sequence of events, such as a story or description of a football match, are narrations.

- *Exposition* is the type of text in which the information is presented as composite concepts, mental constructs, or elements that allow concepts or mental constructs to be analysed. The text provides an explanation of how the component elements interrelate as a meaningful whole. A text that explains the nature of a health problem or discusses the effect of climate change would be an exposition.

- *Argumentation* is the type of text that presents propositions regarding the relationship between concepts or other propositions. An important sub-classification of argument texts is persuasive texts. Examples include newspaper editorials and advertisements.

- *Instruction* (sometimes called *injunction*) is the type of text that provides directions on what to do. Most equipment manuals contain instructional texts, as do other many other guides or handbooks (e.g. a first-aid manual or an introduction to rock climbing).

- *Records* are texts that are designed to standardise, present and conserve information. A table of standings in a sports league is an example of a record, as is a graph of the changes in oil prices. The minutes of a meeting constitute another type of record.

Layout (characteristics of non-continuous texts)

Non-continuous texts differ in terms of their structural organisation as well as their rhetorical features. Five types of non-continuous structures are proposed for PIAAC:[5]

- *Matrix documents*. This set of non-continuous texts consists of four types of increasingly complex documents that have simple lists as their basic unit.

  - A <u>simple list</u> consists of a label and two or more items. The label serves as the organising category and the items all share at least one feature with the other items in the list. Examples include a basic shopping list or a "to do" list.

  - <u>Combined lists</u> consist of two or more simple lists. One list in a combined list is always primary and, as such, ordered to facilitate looking up information within the list and locating parallel information within the other lists. An e-mail inbox, with its related lists of sender names, subjects, dates and file sizes, is an example of the combined list structure.

– <u>Intersected lists</u> are composed of exactly three lists. Two of the lists form a row and column defining the cells that contain the third or intersected list. Television listings are a common example of an intersecting list with the channels and times defining the programme content listed in each cell.

– <u>Nested lists</u> consist of a combination of two or more intersecting lists. In a nested list, one type of information is repeated in each of the intersecting lists. The intersecting list of unemployment rates, for example, may have separate entries under each month for males and females; in this case, gender would be nested under month.

- *Graphic documents.* A major function of graphic documents is to provide a visual summary of quantitative information. Included in this group of texts are pie charts, bar charts and line graphs. While these may appear to be very different types of documents, they all derive from, or can be transformed into, a combined, intersecting or nested list.

- *Locative documents.* Like graphic documents, locative documents or maps portray information visually. Unlike graphic documents that display quantitative information, maps either portray the location of persons, places or things in space, or depict characteristics of different geographic regions (e.g. types of vegetation or characteristics of a population).

- *Entry documents.* Entry documents, or forms, require the reader to provide information that can range from simple to extremely complex. For example, the reader may be asked to check a box, write a single word, number or phrase, or construct a series of phrases or sentences. Generally speaking, forms provide the reader with a label or category for which the reader is asked to provide specifics.

- *Combination documents.* Some displays, especially graphic documents, rely on the use of other types of text for their interpretation. Maps and graphs, for instance, often include legends or other explanatory information in textual form to aid their interpretation.

Features of digital text

Digital texts share the organising principles and rhetorical stances found in continuous and non-continuous texts. However, such texts also have features that distinguish them from paper-and-ink texts, such as navigation tools and linking functions.[6]

- *Hypertext.* Electronic texts may provide direct links to other texts, and it may be necessary to follow these links to gain a full understanding of a topic. Activation of these links is normally achieved by using a mouse to click on a highlighted word or phrase in a text to access another text with (additional) ideas and information relevant to the highlighted part of the passage. Two main types of links are identified:

– *Index-like.* The initial text is a list of topics from which the reader selects one or more for additional information. A common example is a news site on the web that lists headlines on which the reader clicks to view the full stories. Schedules and electronic calendars are another example of an index-like hypertext, as the user can usually click on an entry in a schedule for additional information about that entry.

– *Text-embedded.* In this type of hypertext, a link is embedded in a complete text and the reader is directed to a second text that expands on the immediate topic. A common example of this kind of hypertext is Wikipedia, in which an entry includes many links to other entries or other websites.

- *Interactive.* Electronic texts are often created by a series of authors. E-mails that contain the sequence of the responses of the parties to the exchange are a common example of interactive text. Other examples include comments sections of blogs or other web documents, such as news sites, that allow comments on stories or articles.

- *Other navigation features.* Moving through digital texts typically requires the use of navigation features that are not found in printed texts, such as scroll bars or a mouse to click on a next (or previous) page button.

Social contexts

The circumstances and context in which reading takes place may influence the motivation to read and the manner in which texts are interpreted. Thus, stimulus materials for the assessment must be drawn from a broad range of settings.

- *Work and occupation* includes materials that deal in general with the world of work, such as finding employment, finances and the experience of employment.

- *Personal uses*

  - *Home and family* includes materials that deal with interpersonal relationships, personal finances, housing and insurance.

  - *Health and safety* includes materials that deal with drugs and alcohol, disease prevention and treatment, safety and accident prevention, first aid, emergencies and staying healthy.

  - *Consumer economics* includes materials that deal with credit and banking, savings, advertising, making purchases and maintaining personal possessions.

  - *Leisure and recreation* includes materials that involve travel, recreational activities and restaurants, as well as reading materials for leisure and recreation, itself.

- *Community and citizenship* includes materials that deal with community resources and staying informed.

- *Education and training* includes materials that deal with opportunities for further learning.

ASPECTS OF TASKS

Literacy tasks in the PIAAC assessment are designed to address three broad cognitive strategies identified as necessary for achieving a full understanding of texts:

Access and identify

"Access-and-identify" tasks require the reader to locate items of information in a text. Sometimes it is relatively easy to find the required information, as it is directly and plainly stated in the text. However, access and identify tasks are not necessarily easy. Inferences may have to be made and rhetorical understanding may be required. For instance, identifying the reasons behind a change in a policy by the local government may require an understanding of how those reasons are presented in a text. In IALS and ALL, access-and-identify tasks were described as "locating" (when only one piece of information was required) and "cycling" (when more than one piece of information was required).

Integrate and interpret (relate parts of text to each other)

"Integrate-and-interpret" tasks require the reader to understand the relation(s) between different parts of a text, such as those of problem/solution, cause/effect, category/example, equivalence, compare/contrast and whole/part. These relationships may be explicitly signaled (e.g. the text states that "the cause of X is Y") or may require the reader to make inferences. The text components to be related may be contiguous or may be found in different paragraphs in the same text or in separate documents.

Compare and contrast, two basic evaluation steps, are examples of relating parts of a text to each other. Establishing the basis of a relationship between parts is a form of understanding at the sub-text level. Some parts of a text must be understood in the context of the text as whole since they derive essential elements of their meaning from the larger text.

Readers are sometimes called upon to reach an understanding of a text as a whole. For example, the reader may need to determine the purpose of a text or comprehend its main theme. Sometimes this is made explicit in the text itself with a title, e.g. in an introductory sentence or paragraph. Often, however, readers must discover the purpose or main theme on their own and produce a paraphrase or summary of it.

Evaluate and reflect

"Evaluate-and-reflect" tasks require the reader to draw on knowledge, ideas or values external to the text. The reader must assess the relevance, credibility, argumentation and truthfulness of the information presented in the text within a context of information that is not present in the text. The reader may also evaluate the purposefulness, register, structure or reader-awareness of the text, or the success with which the author uses evidence and language to argue or persuade. Evaluation is particularly important in reading electronic texts where readers must be alert to the text's accuracy, reliability and timeliness.

Readers also need to be aware of the strategies used in texts to persuade them to a particular end, and of the intended audience for the text. Such meta-textual awareness is part of evaluating and reflecting on a text.

FACTORS THAT AFFECT TASK DIFFICULTY

Transparency of the information

An important factor affecting task difficulty is the transparency of the information in the text. A question that explicitly refers to the superficial information (literal information) in the target text is easier to process. For some tasks, the needed information is explicitly signaled; for example, a telephone number always has a particular form and may also be preceded by "Tel" in the text. The text may have a title or the problem and solution may be directly labeled as such.

Degree of complexity in making inferences

- *Paraphrase.* Readers have to process linguistic information by mobilising their lexical and syntactic-semantic knowledge. An example of this is a task requiring readers to find information about the cost of an automobile in a table that uses the word "car" or "auto".

- *High-level text inference.* In a problem/solution text, neither the problem nor the solution need to be explicitly signaled; rather the reader may have to infer what the problem (and/or solution) is from the text itself. The reader cannot necessarily assume that the problem statement will precede the solution.

- *Extra-textual inference.* Some tasks require the reader to bring in information external to the text or from another text in order to understand parts of the text in question. For example, in a notice about local road repair projects, the reader may be expected to apply external knowledge about the local roads in order to understand the repair proposals.

Semantic complexity and syntactic complexity

Studies of both oral and written texts have shown that the more concrete the information is, the easier the task will be. Tasks requiring the reader to identify persons, things or places tend to be easier than those involving abstract properties, such as goals, conditions and purposes. The grammatical structure of the question posed or the stimulus text can also be more or less complex. For instance, negative phrases are more complex than affirmative phrases. The presence of subordinate clauses increases the complexity of syntactic processing.

Amount of information needed

The more information the reader needs from the text to complete the task, the more difficult that task will be. Moreover, the amount of text that must be processed also plays a role in the difficulty of any task.

Prominence of the information

Information located in a prominent location in the text (e.g. in the first or last sentence of a paragraph, in a main, rather than subordinate, clause, at the top or bottom of a list) is easier to access.

Competing information

The more abundant the potentially relevant information that the reader has to sift through to access the needed information, the more difficult the task will be. This is especially true if there is information in the text that might be relevant but is incorrect. If a text includes a telephone number, a fax number and a mobile number, it will be more difficult for the reader to find the fax number than if the text includes only the fax number.

Text features

The degree to which the reader has to construct relations among parts of the text affects the difficulty. Tasks that require the reader to sort out large numbers of anaphoric references or involve text in which text cohesion signals are absent are more difficult.

DISTRIBUTION OF TEST ITEMS BY TASK CHARACTERISTICS

The selection of items included in the PIAAC study was undertaken following the field test, which took place between March and July 2010. The choice was governed by how the items were received in the field test, the need to cover aspects of the assessment frameworks that define the construct, the need to have sufficient linking items to ensure comparability with previous surveys, and the constraints imposed by the adaptive testing design. The distribution of the literacy assessment items included in the PIAAC survey by task characteristics is presented in Tables 3.1-3.3 below. The target distributions identified in the draft framework documents are also presented.

Table 3.1
Distribution of items by medium

	Final item set		Framework goal
	No.	%	%
Print-based texts	30	52	70-80
Digital texts	28	48	20-35
Total	**58**	**100**	**100**

Note: Each category includes continuous, non-continuous and combined texts.

Table 3.2
Distribution of items by contexts

	Final item set		Framework goal
	No.	%	%
Work	10	17	15
Personal	29	50	40
Community	10	23	30
Education	6	10	15
Total	**58**	**100**	**100**

Table 3.3
Distribution by task aspects

	Final item set		Framework goal
	No.	%	%
Access and identify	31	53	40
Integrate and interpret	18	31	45
Evaluate and reflect	9	16	15
Total	**58**	**100**	**100**

LITERACY

EXAMPLES OF ITEMS

Two examples of the types of literacy items used in PIAAC are presented below. Both of these items use print-based stimuli. As all the items using digital stimulus materials (e.g. simulated websites) tested in the PIAAC field test have been included in the final PIAAC instruments, it is not possible to provide examples of this type of item in this document. The sample problem-solving items found later in this document give an idea of the type of "digital" stimulus material used.

The items are presented in the form accessed by respondents taking PIAAC in its CBA form. Respondents answer questions by using a mouse to highlight words and phrases or to click on the appropriate location on the screen.

Literacy – Sample Item 1

This item has a difficulty level of 3 (on a five-point scale) and focuses on the following aspects of the literacy construct:

Cognitive process	*Access and identify*
Context	*Personal*
Medium	*Print*

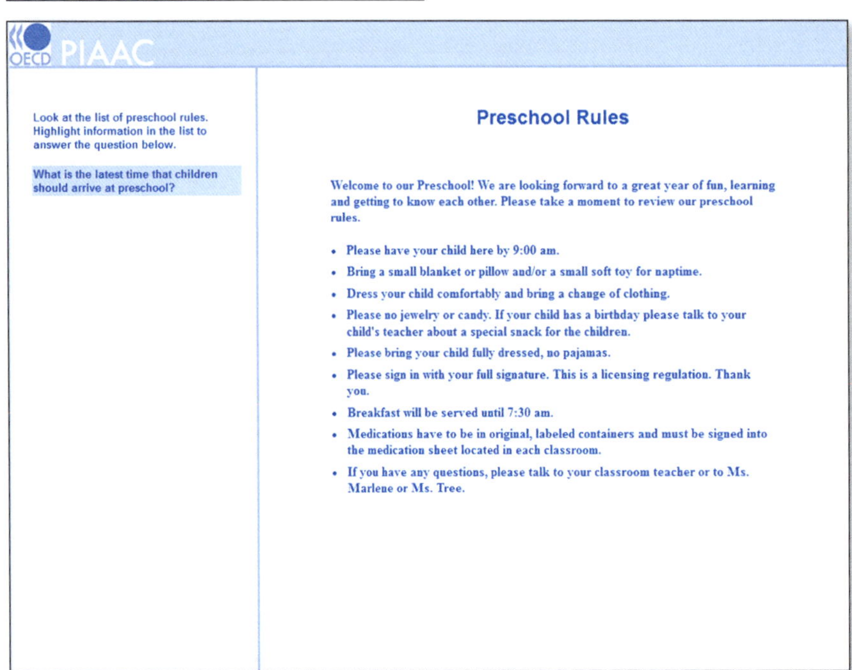

Literacy – Sample Item 2

This item has a difficulty level of 2 and focuses on the following aspects of the literacy construct:

Cognitive process	*Access and identify*
Context	*Personal*
Medium	*Print*

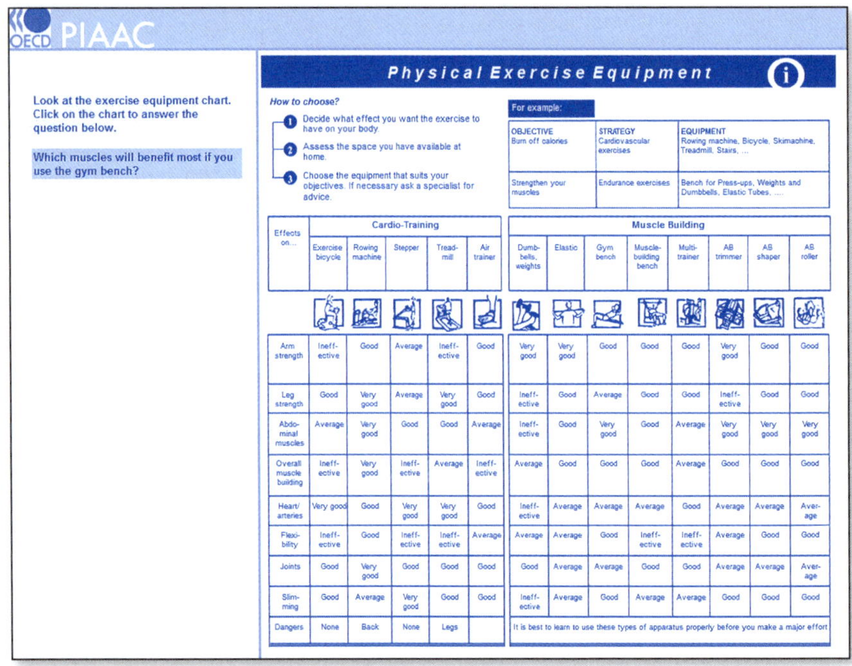

Effects on...	Cardio-Training					Muscle Building							
	Exercise bicycle	Rowing machine	Stepper	Tread-mill	Air trainer	Dumb-bells, weights	Elastic	Gym bench	Muscle-building bench	Multi-trainer	AB trimmer	AB shaper	AB roller
Arm strength	Ineff-ective	Good	Average	Ineff-ective	Good	Very good	Very good	Good	Good	Good	Very good	Good	Good
Leg strength	Good	Very good	Average	Very good	Good	Ineff-ective	Good	Average	Good	Good	Ineff-ective	Good	Good
Abdo-minal muscles	Average	Very good	Good	Good	Average	Ineff-ective	Good	Very good	Good	Average	Very good	Very good	Very good
Overall muscle building	Ineff-ective	Very good	Ineff-ective	Average	Ineff-ective	Average	Good	Good	Good	Average	Good	Good	Good
Heart/ arteries	Very good	Good	Very good	Very good	Good	Ineff-ective	Average	Average	Average	Good	Average	Average	Aver-age
Flexi-bility	Ineff-ective	Good	Ineff-ective	Ineff-ective	Average	Average	Average	Good	Ineff-ective	Ineff-ective	Average	Good	Good
Joints	Good	Very good	Good	Good	Good	Good	Average	Average	Good	Good	Average	Average	Aver-age
Slim-ming	Good	Average	Very good	Good	Good	Ineff-ective	Average	Good	Average	Average	Good	Good	Good
Dangers	None	Back	None	Legs		It is best to learn to use these types of apparatus properly before you make a major effort							

In this item, respondents are asked to answer the question by clicking on the cell in the chart that contains information about exercise equipment. Each of the cells and all of the images are "clickable" and multiple cells can be selected.

Literacy – Sample Item 2, continued

Most of the literacy items have more than one question associated with each stimulus. A second item (also of level 2 difficulty) based on the Exercise Equipment stimulus focuses on the following aspects of the literacy construct:

Cognitive process	*Integrate and interpret*
Context	*Personal*
Medium	*Print*

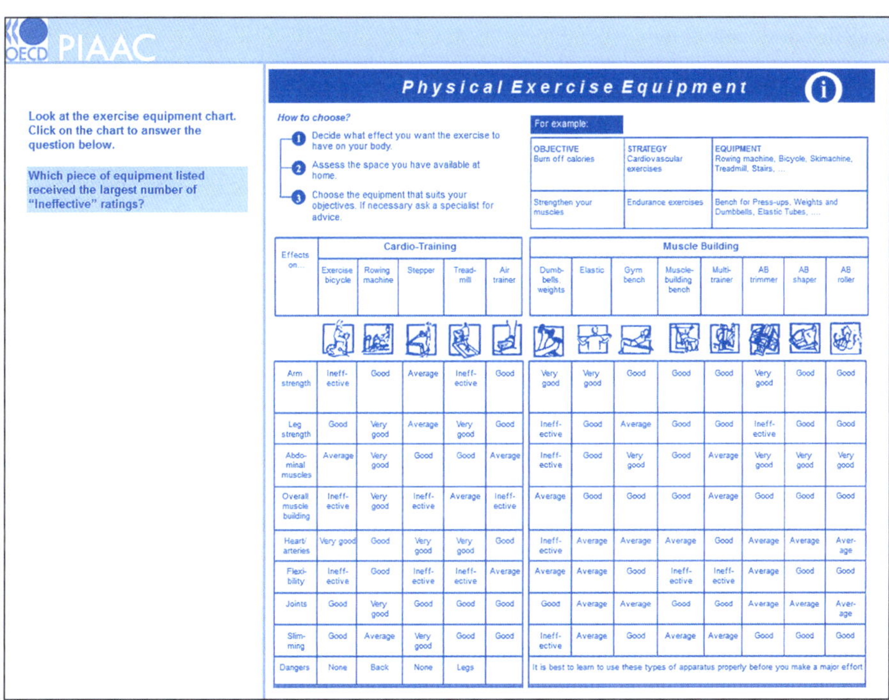

OBJECTIVE	STRATEGY	EQUIPMENT
Burn off calories	Cardiovascular exercises	Rowing machine, Bicycle, Skimachine, Treadmill, Stairs, …
Strengthen your muscles	Endurance exercises	Bench for Press-ups, Weights and Dumbbells, Elastic Tubes, ….

Effects on…	Cardio-Training					Muscle Building							
	Exercise bicycle	Rowing machine	Stepper	Tread-mill	Air trainer	Dumb-bells, weights	Elastic	Gym bench	Muscle-building bench	Multi-trainer	AB trimmer	AB shaper	AB roller
Arm strength	Ineffective	Good	Average	Ineffective	Good	Very good	Very good	Good	Good	Good	Very good	Good	Good
Leg strength	Good	Very good	Average	Very good	Good	Ineffective	Good	Average	Good	Good	Ineffective	Good	Good
Abdominal muscles	Average	Very good	Good	Good	Average	Ineffective	Good	Very good	Good	Average	Very good	Very good	Very good
Overall muscle building	Ineffective	Very good	Ineffective	Average	Ineffective	Average	Good	Good	Good	Average	Good	Good	Good
Heart/arteries	Very good	Good	Very good	Very good	Good	Ineffective	Average	Average	Average	Good	Average	Average	Average
Flexibility	Ineffective	Good	Ineffective	Ineffective	Average	Average	Average	Good	Ineffective	Ineffective	Average	Good	Good
Joints	Good	Very good	Good	Good	Good	Good	Average	Average	Good	Good	Average	Average	Average
Slimming	Good	Average	Very good	Good	Good	Ineffective	Average	Good	Average	Average	Good	Good	Good
Dangers	None	Back	None	Legs		It is best to learn to use these types of apparatus properly before you make a major effort							

READING COMPONENTS

In previous assessments of adult literacy, the information gathered on the reading abilities of adults with poor skills was often insufficient to gain a proper understanding of their difficulties, due to the small number of items at low difficulty levels. To redress this problem, the literacy framework for PIAAC includes a component test intended to provide more information on the abilities of those with low levels of literacy.

The components assessment framework is based on the principle that comprehension – the process of constructing meaning when reading – is built on knowledge of how a given language is represented in its writing system and through component print-reading skills. Evidence of an individual's level of print-reading skills can be captured in tasks that examine a reader's ability and efficiency in processing the elements of the written language, including letters/characters, words, sentences, and larger, continuous segments of text.

A second guiding principle is that the assessment of component skills aims to evaluate the extent to which adults can apply their existing language and comprehension skills to the processing of printed texts. The components tasks are not designed to separately assess the level of language skills in the target writing system and the literacy skills assessed in the main literacy survey. Non-native speakers of the language of the assessment who have only basic oral vocabulary, syntactic/grammatical and linguistic comprehension skills will show poor performance on component reading tasks. As a consequence, low levels of proficiency in the language of the assessment will not be differentiated from low literacy skills in the component tasks.

A third guiding principle is that the levels of proficiency, efficiency and integration of component skills are indicative of the levels of reading development and learning potential. As skills and knowledge accumulate, the ease of processing familiar, text-based print increases. Component efficiency is typically indexed by assessing speed or rate of processing, as well as accuracy.

It is also assumed that the set of component items administered in each country will reflect the linguistic characteristics of the language of assessment. As the relationship of the language to the writing system may be very different in different languages, the nature of the items used to assess the components is being adapted based on consideration of those differences. This best ensures comparability across languages.

Work with this model has typically identified five components:

- alphanumeric perceptual knowledge and familiarity
- word recognition
- word knowledge (vocabulary)
- sentence processing
- passage fluency

The PIAAC components assessment includes tests of vocabulary, sentence processing and basic passage comprehension.

In skilled reading, these components are integrated to support literacy performance. During acquisition, even by adults, they may be measured separately, with different profiles having implications for learning, instruction and policy.

READING COMPONENTS

EXAMPLE OF ITEMS

Examples of the reading-components items are presented below. These items are presented and completed in pencil-and-paper format.

Word meaning (print vocabulary)

In the For Word Meaning items, respondents are asked to circle the word that matches the picture.

<u>Sample 1:</u>

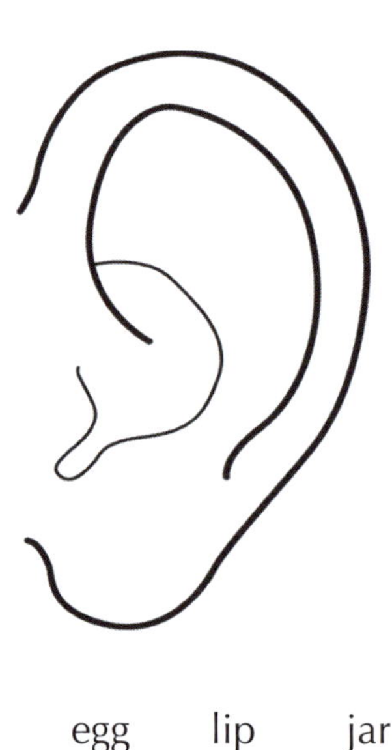

ear   egg   lip   jar

Sample 2:

shoulder   cloud   flower   flag

Sample 3:

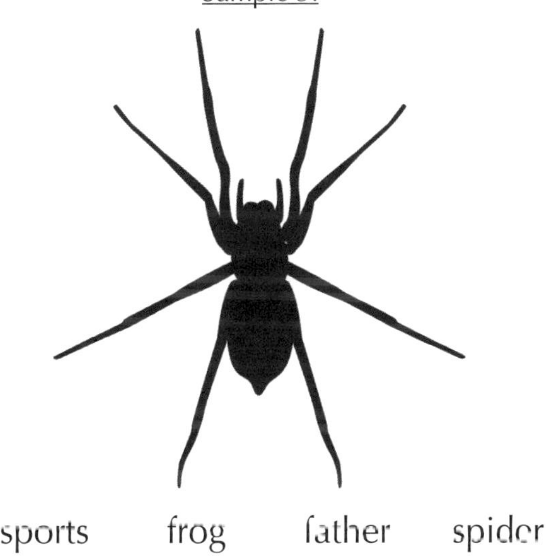

sports   frog   father   spider

Sample 4:

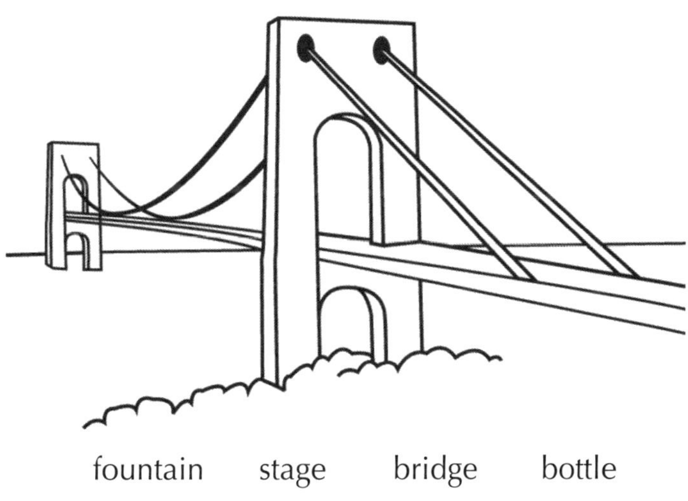

fountain   stage   bridge   bottle

SENTENCE PROCESSING

The sentence-processing items require the respondent to assess whether a sentence makes sense in terms of the properties of the real world or the internal logic of the sentence. The respondent reads the sentence and circles YES if the sentence makes sense or NO if the sentence does not make sense.

Sample sentences:

Three girls ate the song.	YES	NO
The man drove the green car.	YES	NO
The lightest balloon floated in the bright sky.	YES	NO
A comfortable pillow is soft and rocky.	YES	NO
A person who is twenty years old is older than a person who is thirty years old.	YES	NO

PASSAGE COMPREHENSION

The following is an example of an item assessing passage comprehension. Respondents are asked to read a passage and when they come to the underlined alternatives, circle the word that makes sense.

Sample passage:

To the editor: Yesterday, it was announced that the cost of riding the bus will increase. The price will go up by twenty percent starting next <u>wife / month</u>. As someone who rides the bus every day, I am upset by this <u>foot / increase</u>. I understand that the cost of <u>gasoline / student</u> has risen. I also understand that riders have to pay a fair <u>price / snake</u> for bus service. I am willing to pay a little more because I rely on the bus to get to <u>object / work</u>. But an <u>increase / uncle</u> of twenty percent is too much.

This increase is especially difficult to accept when you see the city's plans to build a new sports stadium. The government will spend millions on this project even though we already have a <u>science / stadium</u>. If we delay the stadium, some of that money can be used to offset the increase in bus <u>fares / views</u>. Then, in a few years, we can decide if we really do need a new sports <u>cloth / arena</u>. Please let the city council know you care about this issue by attending the next public <u>meeting / frames</u>.

Notes

1. This is a new feature of the PIAAC framework.

2. Although many .pdf files are simply scanned copies of printed texts, the Acrobat Reader® application adds navigation, search and annotation features not available for the printed version. Thus, a .pdf text would be a digital text according to this definition.

3. There are texts, such as comics and graphic novels, that rely on graphic elements to carry important parts of the information. It seems to us that these are a special case of continuous text where the pictorial displays organise the sequence of ideas somewhat as the ordering of paragraphs does.

4. These are taken almost directly from the IALS and ALL frameworks.

5. This was also the case with the prose and document literacy frameworks of IALS and ALL.

6. These features exist in some standard printed texts, but they are more common in digital texts and are easier to construct and use in their digital form. The use of computer-assisted text layout has also resulted in print texts that are more complex than in the past. Compare a newspaper from the 1960s to one from today to see the impact of this change.

4

Numeracy

This chapter defines PIAAC's concept of numeracy as the ability to access, use, interpret and communicate mathematical information and ideas in order to engage in and manage the mathematical demands of a range of situations in adult life. It describes the principles applied for assessing numeracy in PIAAC and the distribution of the numeracy-assessment items by task characteristics. Sample numeracy items are also provided.

DEFINITION OF THE DOMAIN

PIAAC defines numeracy as *the ability to access, use, interpret and communicate mathematical information and ideas, in order to engage in and manage the mathematical demands of a range of situations in adult life.*

This definition captures essential elements in numerous conceptualisations of numeracy found in the literature. It is compatible with the definition used for ALL and offers a solid basis on which to develop an assessment scale for PIAAC, with its emphasis on competencies in the information age. The inclusion of "engage" in the definition signals that not only cognitive skills but also dispositional elements, i.e. beliefs and attitudes, are necessary for effective and active coping with situations involving numeracy.

Since numeracy is a broad, multifaceted construct referring to a complex competency, the definition of numeracy is coupled with a more detailed definition of *numerate behaviour* and with further specification of the facets of numerate behaviour. This is necessary for the operationalisation of the construct of numeracy in PIAAC and to broaden the understanding of key terms appearing in the definition itself.

Numerate behaviour involves managing a situation or solving a problem in a real context, by responding to mathematical content/information/ideas represented in multiple ways.

Table 4.1

Numerate behaviour – key facets and their components

Numerate behaviour involves managing a situation or solving a problem…

1. In a real context:
- everyday life;
- work;
- society; and
- further learning.

2. By responding:
- identify, locate or access;
- act upon, use: order, count, estimate, compute, measure, model;
- interpret;
- evaluate/analyse; and
- communicate.

3. To mathematical content/information/ideas:
- quantity and number;
- dimension and shape;
- pattern, relationships, change; and
- data and chance.

4. Represented in multiple ways:
- objects and pictures;
- numbers and mathematical symbols;
- formulae;
- diagrams and maps, graphs, tables;
- texts; and
- technology-based displays.

5. Numerate behaviour is founded on the activation of several enabling factors and processes:
- mathematical knowledge and conceptual understanding;
- adaptive reasoning and mathematical problem-solving skills;
- literacy skills;
- beliefs and attitudes;
- numeracy-related practices and experience; and
- context/world knowledge.

FACETS OF NUMERATE BEHAVIOUR

Numerate behaviour is conceived as comprising four facets and several enabling factors.

FACET 1: Contexts

People try to manage or respond to a situation involving numeracy because they want to satisfy a purpose or reach a goal. Four types of contexts that may require the use of numeracy skills are described below. These are not mutually exclusive and may involve the same underlying mathematical themes.

Everyday life

In everyday life, adults encounter quantitative tasks in personal and family contexts or in the pursuit of hobbies, personal development and interests. Representative tasks related to the context of everyday life include: handling money and budgets; shopping and managing personal time; planning travel; playing games of chance; understanding sports scoring and statistics; reading maps; and using measurements in home situations, such as cooking, doing home repairs or pursuing hobbies.

Work-related

At work, adults are confronted with quantitative situations that often are more specialised than those seen in everyday life. Representative tasks related to work situations include: completing purchase orders; totaling receipts; calculating change; managing schedules, budgets and project resources; using spreadsheets; organising and packing different shaped goods; completing and interpreting control charts; making and recording measurements; reading blueprints; tracking expenditures; predicting costs; and applying formulas.

Society or community

Adults need to have an awareness of what is occurring in the society, the economy and the environment (e.g. trends in crime, health, wages, pollution), and may have to take part in social events or community action. This requires a capacity to read and interpret quantitative information presented in the media, including statistical messages and graphs. Adults may also have to manage a variety of situations, such as raising funds for a football club or interpreting the results of a study on a medical condition.

Further learning

Competence in numeracy may enable a person to participate in further study, whether for academic purposes or as part of vocational training. In either case, it is important to know some of the more formal aspects of mathematics that involve symbols, rules and formulae and to understand some of the conventions used to apply mathematical rules and principles.

Performance in all of the above contexts is based on a combination of cognitive and non-cognitive elements; thus numeracy needs to be considered as a competency, not just as the possession of a set of technical skills or know-how. For example, engagement in further learning of mathematical topics, whether in formal or informal contexts, requires the willingness learn in the first place, as well as the capacity to persevere with such learning. For this level of engagement to occur, an adult must have positive beliefs and attitudes about mathematics and about his or her ability to cope with mathematical tasks.

FACET 2: Responses

In real-life situations, people are required to respond to numeracy demands in a variety of ways. Below, types of responses are grouped under three broad headings: Identify, locate, or access; Act upon or use; and Interpret, evaluate/analyse, communicate. While each response is described separately, in real life all three may be present in a dynamic fashion and vary in complexity. Furthermore, responses are shaped not only by the interaction among situational demands, but also by the goals, skills, dispositions and prior practices and experiences of the individual.

Identify, locate, or access

In virtually all situations, people have to identify, locate or access some mathematical information that is present in the task or situation and relevant to their purpose or goal. When it exists alone, this response type often requires a low level of mathematical understanding or the application of simple arithmetic skills. However, this response type is usually found together with the other types of responses listed below.

Act upon or use

In some situations, people must use already-known mathematical procedures and rules or perform actions based on mathematical information identified in the situation. Acting upon or using known methods or information involves arithmetical operations such as counting and making calculations. It may also involve ordering or sorting, estimating or using various measuring devices. Finally, it may involve using (or developing) a formula that serves as a model of a situation or a process.

Interpret, evaluate/analyse, communicate

This response type encompasses three separate but related responses:

- *Interpret.* Some situations do not demand any direct manipulation of or action on available quantitative information, but instead interpretation of the meaning and implications of information of a mathematical or statistical nature. It may be necessary not only to interpret mathematical or statistical information, but also to make a judgment or develop an opinion about it, for example, regarding trends, changes or differences described in a graph, newspaper article or advertisement. Interpretive responses may relate not only to numerical information (i.e. figures or statistical data), but also to broader mathematical or statistical concepts (expressed in oral, textual or visual form), such as rates of change, proportions, distributions, samples, bias, correlation, probability risk and causality.

- *Evaluate/analyse.* This response category is, in part, an extension of the "Interpret" response type. It covers responses to situations in which a person must analyse a problem, evaluate the quality of the solution against some criteria or contextual demands and, if necessary, cycle again through the interpretation, analysis and evaluation stages. Such situations may be encountered in various contexts, including dynamic or information-rich technology environments, or "decision situations". Examples include: processing raw quantitative information through technology-enabled channels (e.g. sifting through a website), and retrieving and integrating information from multiple sources after evaluating their relevance to the task at hand (e.g. compare information from different sources regarding the costs of competing certain courses of action).

- *Communicate.* In addition to the responses listed above, a person may have to represent and communicate mathematical information, describe the results of his or her actions or interpretations to someone else, or explain and justify the logic of his or her analysis or evaluation. This can be done via oral or written means (ranging from presenting a simple number or word, all the way to a detailed explanation); a drawing (a diagram, map, graph); the generation of a computer-based display (e.g. by referencing a spreadsheet-based chart showing the results of "what if" scenarios); or various combinations of these and other modes of communication and illustration.

Problem solving is not conceived as a separate response type, but rather assumed to be part of the demands set forth by the external situation. As is implied in Table 4.2, the goal of numerate behaviour is to manage a situation involving a numeracy task or solve a numeracy-related problem. Hence, several of the response types described above may be called upon and co-occur when people need to solve numeracy-related problems, especially novel ones. Such responses may be aided or organised by more general skills of adaptive reasoning and problem solving, referred to below as "enabling processes" that underlie numerate behaviour.

The main types of responses to mathematical/statistical tasks embedded in a range of real-life situations have been described above. However, a distinction must be made between a conceptual framework and an assessment framework. Not all real-life numeracy tasks can be simulated effectively in an assessment. In addition, the capacity of an assessment to actually *capture, evaluate* and *score* responses associated with numerate behaviour ultimately depends on the technical aspects of that assessment. In particular, tasks requiring communication-based responses, such as explaining interpretations of given information, or describing an evaluation or analysis of a situation or respondents' thinking about that situation, cannot easily be included in PIAAC. Such tasks are an integral component of adult numerate behaviour and are central to the conceptual framework of adult numeracy. However, very few are being included in the item pool for the first cycle of PIAAC.

FACET 3: Mathematical content/information/ideas

Four key areas of mathematical content, information and ideas are covered by the numeracy assessment in PIAAC.

Quantity and number

Quantity is an outgrowth of people's need to quantify the surrounding world. It encompasses attributes such as the number of features or items, prices, size (e.g. length, area and volume), temperature, humidity, atmospheric pressure, populations and growth rates, revenues and profit, etc. *Number* is fundamental to quantification. Different types of numbers constrain quantification in various ways. Whole numbers can serve as counters or estimators; fractions, decimals and percents can offer expressions of greater precision, parts or comparisons; and positive and negative numbers can serve as directional indicators. In addition to quantification, numbers are used as organisers and identifiers (e.g. telephone numbers or postal codes). In calculations, operations (i.e. the four main operations of +, −, x, ÷ and others, such as squaring) are performed on quantities and numbers. Facility with quantity, number and operations on numbers requires a good "sense" of magnitude. Thus, contextual judgment is necessary when deciding how precise one should be or which tool to use (mental arithmetic, a calculator or a computer). Since mathematics is ubiquitous in every adult's life, the good management of money and time depends on a good sense of number and quantity.

Dimension and shape

Dimension includes the "big ideas" related to the description of "things" in space, such as projections, lengths, perimeters, areas, planes, surfaces, location, etc. The capacity to operate with spatial dimensions requires a sense of "benchmarks" and estimation, direct measurement and derived measurement skills. *Shape* involves a category describing real images and entities that can be visualised in two or three dimensions (e.g. houses and buildings, designs in art and craft, safety signs, packaging, snowflakes, knots, crystals, shadows and plants). An awareness of direction and spatial location is a fundamental skill required when reading, interpreting or sketching maps and diagrams. This content area requires an understanding of units and systems of measurement, both informal and standardised, such as the metric and imperial systems.

Pattern, relationships and change

Mathematics is often described as the study of patterns and relationships. *Pattern* covers regularities encountered in the world, such as those in musical forms, nature, traffic, etc. The capacity to analyse and identify patterns and relationships underpins much mathematical thinking. *Relationships* and *change* relate to the mathematics of how things in the world are associated or develop. Individual organisms grow, populations vary over time, prices fluctuate, and moving objects speed up and slow down. Some characteristics or values can change directly in proportion or relation to another change, while other characteristics may change in the opposite direction or in a different way. Change and rates of change describe the evolution of values in time. This domain includes the ability to develop and/or use mathematical formulae relating the different variables involved in a situation, together with the capacity to understand, use and apply a sense of proportional reasoning.

Data and chance

Data and chance encompass two separate but related topics. *Data* covers the "big ideas" related to variability, sampling, error, prediction and statistical topics, such as data collection, data displays and graphs. *Chance* covers the "big ideas" related to probability and relevant statistical methods. Few things in the world are certain; thus, the ability to attach a number to the likelihood of an event is a valuable tool, whether it has to do with the weather, the stock market or the decision to board a plane.

FACET 4: Representations of mathematical information

Mathematical information may be instantiated in many forms. It may be present in the form of entities that can be counted (e.g. people, buildings, cars, etc.); pictures; symbolic notation (e.g. numerals, letters, and operation or relationship signs); formulae, which are models of relationships between entities or variables; visual displays, including diagrams or charts, graphs and tables (used to display aggregate statistical or quantitative information by displaying objects, counting data, etc.) or maps (e.g. of a city or a project plan). A textual element may also communicate mathematical (and statistical) information or affect its interpretation.

Mathematical information may be extracted from various types of *texts*. Two different kinds of text may be encountered in numeracy tasks. The first involves the representation of mathematical information in textual form, i.e. as words or phrases that carry mathematical meaning. Examples include the use of number words (e.g. "five" instead of "5"); basic mathematical terms (e.g. fraction, multiplication, percent, average, proportion); or more complex phrases (e.g. "the crime

rate increased by half") that require interpretation, or coping with double meanings (or with the difference between the mathematical and everyday meanings of the same terms). The second involves cases where mathematical information is expressed in mathematical notations or symbols (e.g. numbers, plus or minus signs, symbols for units of measure, etc.), but is surrounded by text that provides additional information and context. An example is a bank deposit slip with text and instructions, in which numbers describing monetary amounts are embedded.

FACET 5: Enabling processes: cognitive and non-cognitive

Numeracy competence is revealed through individuals' responses (i.e. identifying, interpreting, acting upon, evaluating and communicating) to the mathematical information or ideas represented in a situation or that can be applied to the situation. Numerate behaviour, however, depends not only on cognitive skills or knowledge bases, but also on the enabling factors and processes listed in Table 4.2.

These enabling processes involve the integration of mathematical knowledge and conceptual understanding of broader reasoning, problem-solving skills, and literacy skills. Furthermore, numerate behaviour and autonomous engagement with numeracy tasks depend on the dispositions (beliefs, attitudes, habits of minds, etc), prior experiences and practices that an adult brings to each situation.

Mathematical knowledge and conceptual understanding

Conceptual understanding refers to *an integrated and functional grasp of mathematical ideas*. Conceptual understanding can help learners to produce reasonable estimates that can, in turn, help them to catch computational errors, realise that a particular product is not necessary, or estimate enough for the purpose. This kind of understanding also obviates the necessity to rely on memory for all methods and procedures: i.e. an adult can think about the meaning of the task at hand and "construct or reconstruct" a representation that illustrates both what it means and suggests as a method for solution.

Adaptive reasoning and problem-solving skills

Adults develop and apply diverse strategies to manage quantitative situations. Some may be based on prior formal learning, while others may be based on personal experience or adapted to fit the situation at hand. To solve computational problems or manage certain quantitative tasks, people have to re-construct reality in a mathematical way, for example, by modeling or mathematising. They can do so either alone or in conjunction with others. Problem-solving strategies may include: extracting relevant information from the task/activity; rewriting/restating the task; drawing pictures, diagrams or sketches; guessing and checking; making a table; and/or generating a concrete model or representation.

Literacy skills

Reading, writing and oral communication are important skills in undertaking a numeracy task or activity or communicating the outcomes of such tasks. When "mathematical representations" involve text, performance on numeracy tasks depend not only on formal mathematical or statistical knowledge but also on reading comprehension and literacy skills, reading strategies and prior literacy experiences.

Context and world knowledge

Appropriately interpreting mathematical information or quantitative messages depends on the ability to place messages in a context of knowledge about the world or personal experiences and practices. World knowledge complements literacy skills and is critical for interpreting any message. For example, adults' ability to make sense of statistical claims made in the media in part depends on the information they can glean about the origin and nature of the study or data being discussed.

Beliefs and attitudes

Research suggests that the way in which a person responds to a numeracy task depends not only on knowledge and skills but also on attitudes towards mathematics, beliefs about mathematical skills, habits of mind, and prior experiences involving tasks with mathematical content. Some adults, including highly educated ones, decide that they are not "good with numbers" or have other negative feelings towards mathematics. Such attitudes and beliefs stand in contrast to the desired sense of being "at home with numbers" and can interfere with the motivation to develop new mathematical skills or tackle mathematics-related tasks, and may also affect test performance.

Adults with a negative mathematical self-concept may elect to avoid a problem with quantitative elements, address only a portion of it, or delegate it to someone else by asking a family member or salesperson for help. Such decisions or actions can serve to reduce both mental and emotional loads, but fall short of autonomous engagement with the mathematical demands of real-world tasks and carry negative consequences.

Numeracy-related practices and experiences

Mathematical knowledge is developed in many situations and not only through formal education. Saxe (1992) and his colleagues (Saxe, et al., 1996) have written about the importance of cultural practice in the development of mathematical thinking, and how such practices profoundly influence an individual's cognitive constructions of mathematical ideas. The frequency of engagement with mathematical tasks or of exposure to mathematical or statistical information or displays, whether at work, home, when shopping, or in other contexts, is also important. The level of engagement and exposure may be the outcome of competence, but may also be a reason for observed skills levels or, at a minimum, a factor influencing observed skills levels independent of formal schooling.

Numerate behaviour does not only rely on mathematical knowledge or related reasoning and problem-solving skills acquired as part of formal learning in a school context. Attitudes and beliefs, as well as numeracy-related practices and world knowledge, are important enabling processes and may influence adults' ability to act in a numerate way.

PRINCIPLES FOR ASSESSING NUMERACY IN PIAAC

The development of the numeracy assessment for PIAAC was based on a number of general principles or guidelines listed below:

- *Items should cover as many aspects as possible within each of the four facets of the numeracy competency.* Items should require the activation of a broad range of skills and knowledge included in the construct of numeracy.

- *Items should aspire to maximal authenticity and cultural appropriateness.* Tasks should be derived from real-life stimuli and pertain to all types of contexts or situations (i.e. everyday life, work, society, further learning) that can be expected to be of importance or relevance in the countries participating in PIAAC. Item content and questions should appear purposeful to respondents across cultures. With that said, it must be acknowledged that in a large-scale assessment such as PIAAC, not all items and contexts will be personally familiar to all adults within any one country, let alone across all countries.

- *Items should have a free-response format, to the extent feasible by the computer platform used for administering the direct assessments.* Items should be structured to include a stimulus (e.g. a picture, drawing, visual display) and one or more questions, the answers to which the respondent communicates via the modes available within the test platform, primarily: numeric entry; click; highlight a region of the stimulus; or use of various pull-down menus. In addition, items allowing a free-form response should be used in the paper-and-pencil portion of PIAAC.

- *Items should spread over different levels of ability.* Items should span the range of ability levels anticipated among PIAAC participants, from low-skilled individuals to those with advanced competencies.

- *Items should represent the different response types.* Certain types of numeracy responses, especially those requiring the use of interpretation, evaluation, analysis and communication, is receiving only partial coverage in the first cycle of PIAAC due to the constraints associated with computer-based assessment platforms.

- *Items should vary in the degree to which the task is embedded in text.* Some items should use relatively rich texts while others should use little or no text. This distribution aims to reflect the different levels of text involvement in real-world numeracy tasks, as well as minimise overlap with the literacy assessment.

- *Items should be efficient.* To allow for coverage of many key facets of the numeracy competency, a large number of diverse stimuli and questions are being included. However, given testing-time constraints, the use of short tasks is necessary, precluding items that can simulate extended problem-solving processes or require a lengthy open-ended response.

- *Items should be adaptable to unit systems across participating countries.* Items should be designed in a way that their underlying mathematical demands are as consistent as possible across countries, regardless of language and mathematical conventions. After being translated, items should retain equivalency with respect to their mathematical or cognitive demands.

The distribution of the numeracy-assessment items included in the PIAAC survey by task characteristics is presented in Tables 4.2-4.4 below. The target distributions identified in the draft framework documents are also presented.

Table 4.2
Distribution of items by response (process)

	Final item set		Framework goal
	No.	%	%
Act upon, use	34	61	50
Identify, locate or access	3	5	10
Interpret, evaluate	19	34	40
Total	**56**	**100**	**100**

Note: Each category includes continuous, non-continuous and combined texts.

Table 4.3
Distribution of items by contexts

	Final item set	
	No.	%
Everyday life	25	45
Work-related	13	23
Society and community	14	25
Further learning	4	7
Total	**56**	**100**

Table 4.4
Distribution of items by mathematical content

	Final item set		Framework goal
	No.	%	%
Data and chance	12	21	25
Dimension and shape	16	29	25
Pattern, relationships and change	15	27	20
Quantity and change	13	23	30
Total	**55**	**100**	**100**

NUMERACY

EXAMPLES OF ITEMS

Four examples of numeracy items are shown below. They are presented in the form accessed by respondents taking PIAAC in its CBA form. Respondents answer questions by using a mouse to click on the appropriate location on the screen or by tying responses in the space provided.

Numeracy – Sample Item 1

This sample item (of difficulty level 3) focuses on the following aspects of the numeracy construct:

Content	*Data and chance*
Process	*Interpret, evaluate*
Context	*Community and society*

Respondents are asked to respond by clicking on one or more of the time periods provided in the left pane on the screen.

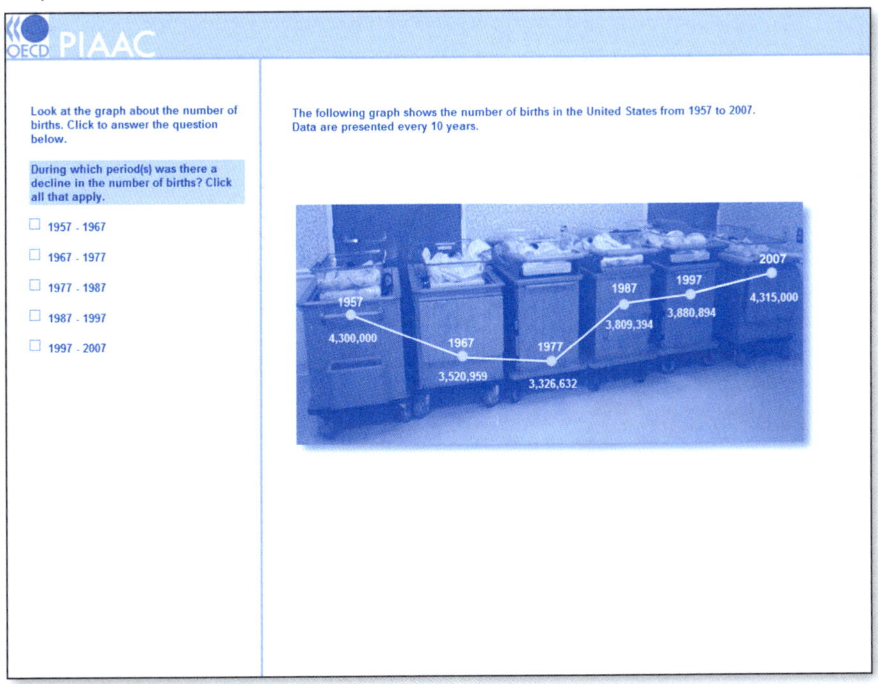

Correct Response: 1957 - 1967 and 1967 – 1977

Numeracy – Sample Item 2

This sample item (of difficulty level 3) focuses on the following aspects of the numeracy construct:

Content	*Dimension and shape*
Process	*Act upon, use (estimate)*
Context	*Every day or work*

Respondents are asked to type in a numerical response based on the graphic provided.

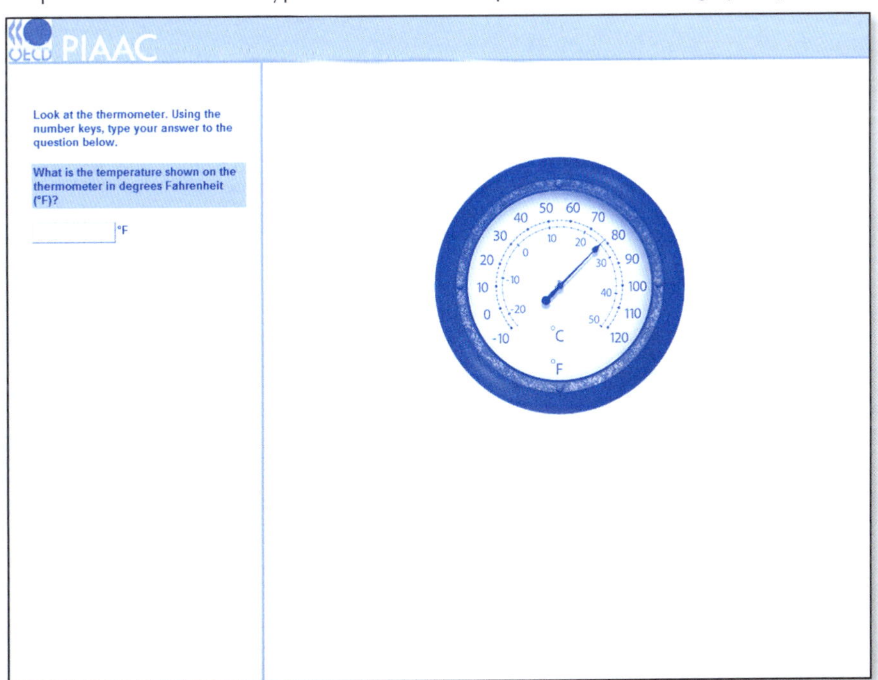

Correct Response: Any value between 77.7 and 78.3

Numeracy – Sample Item 3

This third item (of difficulty level 1) in the set focuses on the following aspects of the numeracy construct:

Content	*Dimension and shape*
Process	*Act upon, use (measure)*
Context	*Every day or work*

Respondents are asked to type in a numerical response based on the graphic provided.

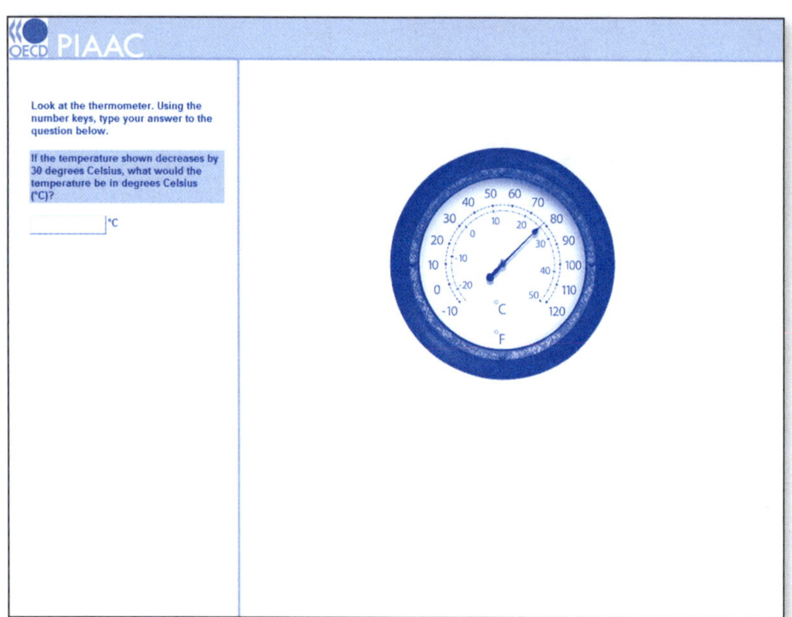

Correct Response: Any value between -4 and -5

Numeracy – Sample Item 4

This sample item (of difficulty level 4) focuses on the following aspects of the numeracy construct:

Content	*Quantity and Number*
Process	*Act upon, use (compute)*
Context	*Community and society*

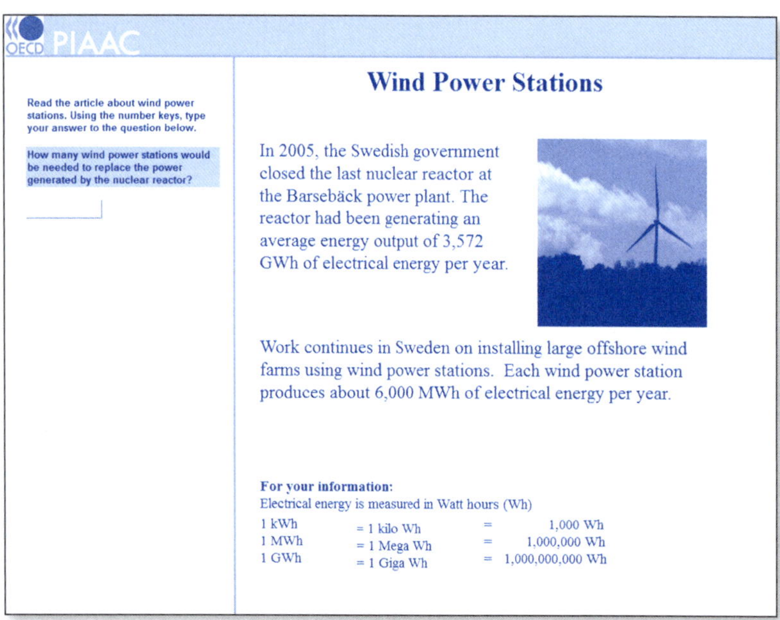

Correct Response: Any value between 23 and 24

References

Saxe, G. B. (1992), *Culture and Cognitive Development: Studies in Mathematical Understanding*, Lawrence Erlbaum Associates, Hillsdale, New Jersey.

Saxe, G. B., V. Dawson, R. Fall, and **S. Howard** (1996), "Culture and Children's Mathematical Thinking", in R. Sternberg and T. Ben-Zeev (eds.), *The Nature of Mathematical Thinking* (pp. 119-144), Lawrence Erlbaum Associates, Hillsdale, New Jersey.

5

Problem Solving in Technology–Rich Environments

This chapter defines PIAAC's concept of problem solving in technology-rich environments, including the specific kinds of problems people confront when using information and communication technologies. Sample items to measure adults' ability to solve problems in technology-rich environments are provided.

DEFINITION OF THE DOMAIN

Problems and problem solving

A problem is usually defined as a situation where a person cannot immediately and routinely achieve his or her goals due to some kind of obstacle or challenge. The ability to solve problems is considered to be one of the most complex and sophisticated aspects of human cognition. In order to solve a problem, individuals must first become aware of a difference between the current state of affairs and the state of affairs that corresponds to the satisfaction of their goals. In other words, they must come to an understanding of the nature of the problem. This is also called "problem finding". Individuals then need to engage in a series of thought processes and concrete actions in order to define a set of sub-goals and steps through which the problem may be solved (also called planning or "problem shaping"), and perform the actions required to attain those sub-goals until the situation reaches a satisfactory state. Throughout the problem-solving activity, individuals must monitor their progress and, where necessary, reconsider their goals and actions. For instance, individuals may face an unexpected outcome or find themselves at an impasse. In such cases, they may have to reconsider their understanding of the problem or the actions they have decided to take in order to solve the problem.

Problem solving also normally requires the use of a range of tools and information resources. Tools and technologies normally facilitate the resolution of the problem. They may, however, add to the difficulty of a problem, especially when a person has limited knowledge and experience using the given tools and technologies.

In concrete, everyday situations, problems and problem solving often involve interaction with other individuals. A person may be asked to solve a problem for another person and may need to receive information or advice from another person, or may want to communicate the solution to someone else. Communicating in spoken or written form (e.g. comprehending instructions, asking questions or explaining) may be one of the actions necessary to solve the problem. Thus, communication skills must be considered a factor in assessing problem-solving skills. In technology-rich environments, several powerful tools for rapid (e.g. e-mail and chat software) and broad (e.g. blogs, shared applications) communication are available, thus enabling collaborative problem-solving activities for many people in different locations. Such tools require special skills for computer-mediated communication.

From a cognitive perspective, problem solving involves a complex hierarchy of processes and skills. The core characteristic of problem solving is that it is impossible for a person to achieve the goal through routine actions. In problem solving, one has to reflect on the situation in order to identify the proper arrangement of decisions and actions that may lead to a solution. Thus, the status of problems is conditional and based on a person's familiarity with the problem or category of problems. Some activities initially experienced as problem solving may become routine activities over time with learning and practice.

Regardless of a person's ability level, some problems are intrinsically more complex than others. Dimensions of problem complexity include: the clarity of the initial situation; the number of sub-goals and steps needed to solve the problem; the amount of information to be considered; and the pragmatic constraints that surround the person's activity (e.g. time constraints, level of stakes or hazard, probability of unexpected events or outcomes, etc). The complexity of a problem also varies as a function of the arrangement of informational and other resources in the problem-solving environment.

Research on problem solving has also established distinctions between types of problems. One important distinction is between closed and open problems. In closed problems, the resources (e.g. objects, tools) available and the range of possible actions are limited. An example is a chess game in which the possible moves are limited by the size of the chessboard and the rules of the game. In other problems, the potential resources and possible actions are, in principle, unlimited. Finding one's way in an unfamiliar city or designing a new kitchen may be considered open problems.

Another important distinction is between well-defined and ill-defined problems. Well-defined problems provide a clear solution path. There is no straightforward link, however, between the definition of a problem and its absolute level of difficulty. Sometimes ill-defined problems are easy to solve because they allow several solution paths. That said, ill-defined problems also require the problem solver to set up appropriate sub-goals and operators and select appropriate resources, which may increase the difficulty of the problem.

Information problems

The PS-TRE (problem solving in technology-rich environments) domain of PIAAC covers the specific class of problems people deal with when using ICT. These problems share the following characteristics:

- The existence of the problem is primarily a consequence of the availability of new technologies. One example relates to the vast amount of information now available on the World Wide Web, including specialist knowledge that can be accessed by laypersons. This gives rise to problems related to locating and evaluating information for quality and credibility (e.g. when seeking advice about legal issues or medical conditions). The evaluation and critical judgment of information are core aspects of literate Internet use and is one focus of the PS-TRE assessment.

- The solution to the problem requires the use of computer-based artifacts (tools, representational formats, computational procedures). An example is the management of personal finances using spreadsheets, statistical packages and graphical tools. Here, the problem itself may not be new (e.g. keeping spending and income in balance), but the new artifacts modify the distribution of work across social agents (professionals vs. laypersons) and transform the procedures and steps required to solve the problem.

- The problems are related to the handling and maintenance of technology-rich environments themselves (e.g. how to operate a computer, how to fix a settings problem, how to use the Internet browser in a technical sense).

Most of the problems corresponding to these broad characteristics require the handling of vast amounts of symbolic information and an ability to deal with semantic content or meaning. Examples include understanding command names in drop-down menus, the naming of files and folders, hits in a search engine, or links in a web page. Many problems also require the person to read and understand electronic texts, graphics and numerical data. Therefore, understanding and evaluating meaningful information available in technology-rich environments is central to the construct of PS-TRE.

Defining problem solving in technology-rich environments

In PIAAC, problem solving in technology-rich environments is defined as:

> *using digital technology, communication tools and networks to acquire and evaluate information, communicate with others and perform practical tasks. The first PIAAC problem-solving survey focuses on the abilities to solve problems for personal, work and civic purposes by setting up appropriate goals and plans, and accessing and making use of information through computers and computer networks.*

Each sentence in the definition serves a specific purpose. The first is aimed at providing a broad basis for the initial and subsequent assessments of PS-TRE; the second acknowledges the existence of constraints limiting the scope of the first wave of PIAAC. A more detailed elaboration of the elements of the definition is offered below.

Using digital technology, communication tools and networks

PIAAC focuses on problems that are specifically related to the use of ICT. While the problem-solving context refers to routine or basic ICT skills, they are not central to the framework. PS-TRE focuses on situations that involve the user's active construction of goals and strategies. Given the increasing diversity and versatility of digital technologies, a full assessment of PS-TRE should not be limited to traditional desktop computing. Mobile and integrated technologies may be involved in new types of problem solving and will need to be represented in future assessments.

Acquire and evaluate information

Most uses of digital technologies involve work with symbolic information, such as texts, graphics, links and commands. Symbolic information is used as a part of human-computer interfaces (e.g. icons, commands) and it constitutes the primary content of most computer applications (e.g. word processor, spreadsheet, Internet browser and e-mail applications).

Communicate with others

Digital technologies provide powerful and flexible means for people to communicate with each other. Examples include e-mail, chats, short-message systems and IP audio-visual communication. Digital communication may take place in the context of purposeful, problem-like situations and, therefore, it is an integral part of the PS-TRE construct in PIAAC.

Perform practical tasks

The ability to solve problems with digital technologies is linked to the achievement of personal, civic and work-related goals, which, in turn, take the form of concrete, practical tasks. Examples include shopping, learning about laws and regulations, and organising teamwork through online agendas and reservation systems. The problems assessed in PIAAC use authentic, meaningful scenarios based on surveys of computer uses and input from participating countries.

The first PIAAC problem-solving survey

PIAAC represents the first attempt to assess PS-TRE on a large scale and as a single dimension. This creates many challenges regarding the definition of tasks and the practical collection of data. Furthermore, digital technologies continue to evolve at a rapid pace, as do the personal, social and work-related uses of these technologies. While setting the stage for further rounds of assessment, the present framework takes into consideration issues of feasibility as well as the possible evolution of technology and its uses.

Focuses on the abilities to solve problems for personal, work and civic purposes

In order to reflect the pervasiveness of ICT in the society, PIAAC PS-TRE assesses problem-solving abilities based on scenarios that pertain to these three important contexts (personal, work and civic contexts).

By setting up appropriate goals and plans

An assessment of problem-solving capacities should focus on situations where test takers cannot immediately reach their goal based on routine, mechanical sets of actions. Thus, the focus is on tasks that require test takers to actively construct a solution based on the resources available in the assessment environment.

Accessing and making use of information

This phrase emphasises a specific aspect of PS-TRE, namely that the assessment focuses on information-rich problems that require individuals to access, interpret and integrate multiple sources of information.

Through computers and computer networks

"Technology-rich environments" encompass more than just personal computers. A full assessment of problem solving in TRE would require the simulation of the diversity and versatility of today's digital technologies. However, for reasons of feasibility, the first assessment is being restricted to problems requiring the use of computers and Internet-based services.

CORE DIMENSIONS OF PROBLEM SOLVING IN TECHNOLOGY-RICH ENVIRONMENTS

The domain of PS-TRE is conceived along three dimensions (see Figure 5.1).

■ Figure 5.1 ■
Core dimensions of problem solving in technology-rich environments

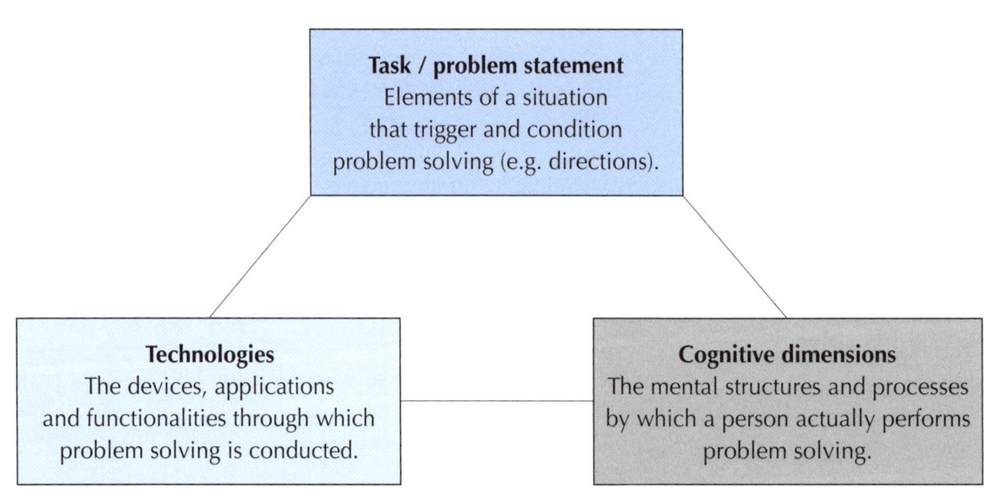

"Cognitive dimensions" includes the mental structures and processes involved when a person solves a problem. These include setting goals and monitoring progress; planning; locating, selecting and evaluating information; and organising and transforming information.

"Technologies" are the devices, applications and functionalities through which problem solving is conducted. These include hardware devices (laptop computers in the case of PIAAC); simulated software applications; commands and functions; and representations (text, graphics, etc.).

"Tasks" are the circumstances that trigger a person's awareness and understanding of the problem and determine the actions needed to be taken in order to solve the problem. Ordinarily, a wide range of conditions can initiate problem solving. For instance, a computer user may realise that his or her mailbox is crowded and that a new schema is needed for classifying e-mails. Alternatively, he or she may be faced with a complex issue (such as finding out more about a medical treatment) and decide to look for relevant information on the Web. In test-taking contexts, tasks are more explicitly assigned to participants. They include the question and task instructions presented to test takers, as well as the specific materials and time constraints associated with the test.

Cognitive dimensions

Table 5.1 summarises the cognitive dimensions of problem solving that are being assessed in PIAAC. These dimensions are: setting goals and monitoring progress; planning and self-organisation; acquiring and evaluating information; and using information.

Table 5.1
Cognitive dimensions in PS-TRE

Dimension	Examples
Setting goals and monitoring progress	- Identifying one's needs or purposes, given the explicit and implicit constraints of a situation - Establishing and applying criteria for constraint satisfaction and achievement of a solution - Monitoring progress - Detecting and interpreting unexpected events, impasses and breakdowns
Planning, self-organising	- Setting up adequate plans, procedures and strategies (operators) - Selecting appropriate devices, tools or categories of information
Acquiring and evaluating information	- Orienting and focusing one's attention - Selecting information - Assessing reliability, relevance, adequacy, comprehensibility - Reasoning about sources and contents
Using information	- Organising information, integrating across potentially inconsistent texts and across formats, making informed decisions - Transforming information through writing, from text to table, from table to graph, etc. - Communicating with relevant parties

Technology dimensions

Table 5.2 summarises the technology dimensions that are taken into account in PIAAC. Hardware devices include artifacts that rely on digital technologies, such as desktop or laptop computers, mobile phones, and so forth. These devices are increasingly incorporated into other devices, such as cars or kitchen appliances; hence the phrase "integrated digital technologies" is used. It is important to note that, in the first cycle of the assessment, only laptop computers with simulated software applications are being included. In addition, for operational reasons, sound, animations and videos are not being used. However, the general definition above provides for the inclusion of other digital devices in future cycles.

In addition to artifacts, technology-rich environments involve the use of software applications. In turn, these applications rely on commands, functions and representations of information. Commands and functions are differentiated from applications as some commands and functions are found across a broad range of applications. It is unclear if the knowledge of the use of these commands is linked to familiarity with the particular applications in which they are found.

Examples include "sort" or "find" commands. Similarly, texts, graphics and other representations exist independently of the specific applications in which they are found.

Table 5.2
Technology dimensions of PS-TRE

Dimension	Examples
Hardware devices	Desktop or laptop computers, mobile phones, personal assistants, global positioning systems, integrated digital devices
Software applications	File management, web browser, e-mail, spreadsheet
Commands, functions	Buttons, links, textboxes, copy/cut/paste, sort, find
Representations	Texts, sound, numbers, graphics (fixed or animated), video

Note: Only laptop devices, a few simulated software applications and a restricted range of representations are being included in the first cycle of PIAAC.

Task dimensions

Table 5.3 summarises the dimensions of the tasks that are being assessed in PIAAC PS-TRE. These include: the purpose; the context in which each task is performed; the intrinsic complexity of the problem; and the explicitness of the problem statement and task directions given to the test taker.

Table 5.3
Task dimensions in PS-TRE

Dimension	Examples
Task purposes (contexts)	Personal, work/occupation, civic
Intrinsic complexity	Minimal number of steps required to solve the problem Number of options or alternatives at various stages Diversity of operators required, complexity of computation/transformation Likelihood of impasses or unexpected outcomes Number of constraints to be satisfied Amount of transformation required to communicate a solution
Explicitness of problem statement	Ill-defined (implicit, unspecified) vs. well-defined (explicit, described in detail)

Intrinsic complexity

The "intrinsic complexity" of a problem is related to a set of more specific variables: the minimum number of steps or actions required to solve the problem; the number of options at each phase; the diversity of operators and the complexity of mental reasoning and/or computation; the probability of impasses or unexpected outcomes; the number of constraints to be satisfied; and the amount of composition or transformation needed to communicate a solution.

Number of steps or sub-goals required to reach a solution

Tasks that present a problem with a single goal and few required steps are likely to be easier than those with multiple goals or sub-goals that require a number of steps to reach a solution.

Probability of impasses or unexpected outcomes

Tasks with unanticipated impasses or outcomes are expected to be more difficult than those without. One advantage of computer-delivered assessments lies in the possibility of designing tasks in which additional constraints or outcomes can be introduced as a test taker works through them. For example, at a defined point in a task, an unexpected e-mail might appear and add new information that test takers must consider while working towards solving the initial problem.

Amount of transformation and generation required to communicate a solution

Tasks requiring test takers to represent or compose information to convey a solution are likely to be more difficult than tasks requiring more defined responses. Tasks of transformation and generation include constructing a table, re-representing text in a graph, or writing a justification. In order to keep the PS-TRE framework distinct from the numeracy framework, however, these tasks do not include the production of statistical graphs. Writing lengthy open justifications is also not required, due to difficult scoring issues. Nevertheless, participants may be asked to evaluate the communicative effectiveness of a graph or to select among several possible justifications.

Specificity and explicitness of task constraints

It is expected that tasks that explicitly define the problem to be solved and the steps required to reach a solution will be easier than tasks that present ill-defined problems. A problem situation that requires the test taker to select operators and sub-goals or define the successful achievement of a goal makes the problem more difficult.

PROBLEM SOLVING IN TECHNOLOGY-RICH ENVIRONMENTS IN RELATION TO OTHER DOMAINS OF PIAAC

The constructs of literacy, numeracy and PS-TRE rely on the same "core" cognitive processes. For example, tasks in all three of these domains require both an ability to decode printed symbols and a minimal working memory capacity. PS-TRE also assesses a set of competencies distinct from those defined in the other two constructs.

The assessment of PS-TRE in PIAAC focuses on goal setting, monitoring and planning in technology-rich environments, and assessment tasks emphasise the problem-finding and problem-shaping processes typically found in these environments. Tasks include: selecting an appropriate software application; deciding on one among several possible strategies; making use of adequate functionalities in a context-sensitive manner; interpreting ill-structured texts; and using online forms.

Problem-solving tasks are being carried out in environments that involve multiple and complex sources of information. Some of the tasks require the test taker to use and shift across multiple environments. PS-TRE therefore assesses decision making with respect to the use of information sources (for example, choosing which environment to use or deciding whether or not to go to another website.) Evaluation is being included as a critical underlying part of problem solving. Additionally, the selection of appropriate devices or tools is taking a prominent role in this domain.

In terms of processing information, problem solving is a specific construct in that it focuses on:

- The evaluation of sources in terms of reliability and the adequacy of information relative to the problem statement, as opposed to mere topical relevance, which is more applicable for literacy.

- The integration of information across sources, especially in cases where the sources provide inconsistent information.

PS-TRE tasks are seeking to mimimise the numeracy and literacy demands placed on test takers in order to increase the specificity and validity of the construct.

PROBLEM SOLVING IN TECHNOLOGY-RICH ENVIRONMENTS AND ICT COMPETENCE

What differentiates the problem-solving domain from the general ICT domain? ICT skills may be broadly defined as "the interest, attitude, and ability of individuals to appropriately use digital technology and communication tools" (Lennon, et al., 2003). As is true for literacy and numeracy skills, ICT skills underlie PS-TRE. However, the PS-TRE construct aims to encompass more than the purely instrumental skills related to the knowledge and use of digital technologies. The cognitive dimensions of problem solving are considered the central object of the assessment, with the use of ICT as secondary.

Prerequisite skills

PS-TRE tasks presuppose the mastery of foundational ICT skills. These include the manipulation of input and output devices (e.g. the mouse, keyboard and digital displays), an awareness of concepts including files and folders, and an understanding of basic file-management operations, such as save, open, close, delete, move and rename. In addition, test takers should be at least minimally familiar with simple graphic interface features, such as the iconic representations of files and folders, hyperlinks, scrollbars and different types of menus and buttons.

Task characteristics

Fourteen problem-solving items are included in the PIAAC assessment. These involve both short and long scenarios.

The short scenarios represent the most direct and least complex of the tasks in the assessment. In these scenarios, a test taker may be given a simulated page of hits from an Internet search and be asked to evaluate the choices and select one that meets a short list of specified criteria.

The ten-minute scenarios involve multiple steps and, in some cases, multiple technology environments. Test takers may be presented with a problem that requires them to locate an e-mail message, open an attachment, and then use information in the attachment to create a brief table that can represent the information for a specific purpose.

The 15-minute scenarios have been designed to simulate real-life problem-solving activities that are recursive and more exploratory in nature. The tasks often cross multiple environments and require test takers to employ several, if not all, of the cognitive components. A sample complex scenario would involve a test taker conducting a search in a simulated web environment, integrating and evaluating information across a number of sites, and then using the information to generate a summary to be shared as part of a community presentation.

The distribution of the literacy assessment items included in the PIAAC assessment by task characteristics is presented in Tables 5.4-5.9 below.

Table 5.4
Distribution of tasks as a function of cognitive dimensions

Dimension	No.*
Setting goals and monitoring progress	4
Planning	7
Acquiring and evaluating information	8
Using information	6

*Does not add up to 14 as some tasks are coded to more than one dimension.

Table 5.5
Distribution of tasks as a function of technology dimensions

Dimension	No.*
Web	7
Spreadsheet	7
E-mail	4

*Does not add up to 14 as some tasks are coded to more than one dimension.

Table 5.6
Distribution by context

Dimension	No.
Personal	8
Work / Occupation	4
Civic	2

Table 5.7
Distribution by intrinsic complexity (number of steps)

Dimension	No.
Single step	8
Multiple steps	6

Table 5.8
Distribution by intrinsic complexity (number of constraints)

Dimension	No.
Single constraint	7
Multiple constraints	7

Table 5.9
Distribution by explicitness of problem statement

Dimension	No.
Ill-defined problem statement	7
Well-defined problem statement	7

PROBLEM SOLVING IN TECHNOLOGY-RICH ENVIRONMENTS
EXAMPLES OF ITEMS

Two examples of PS-TRE items are presented below. These items can be administered in electronic format only. Examples of items are only available in print layout.

Sample Item 1

In this item (of level 4 difficulty), respondents must access and evaluate information in the context of a simulated job search. The instructions, located on the left side of the screen, require respondents to identify and then bookmark one or more sites that do not require users to register or pay a fee.

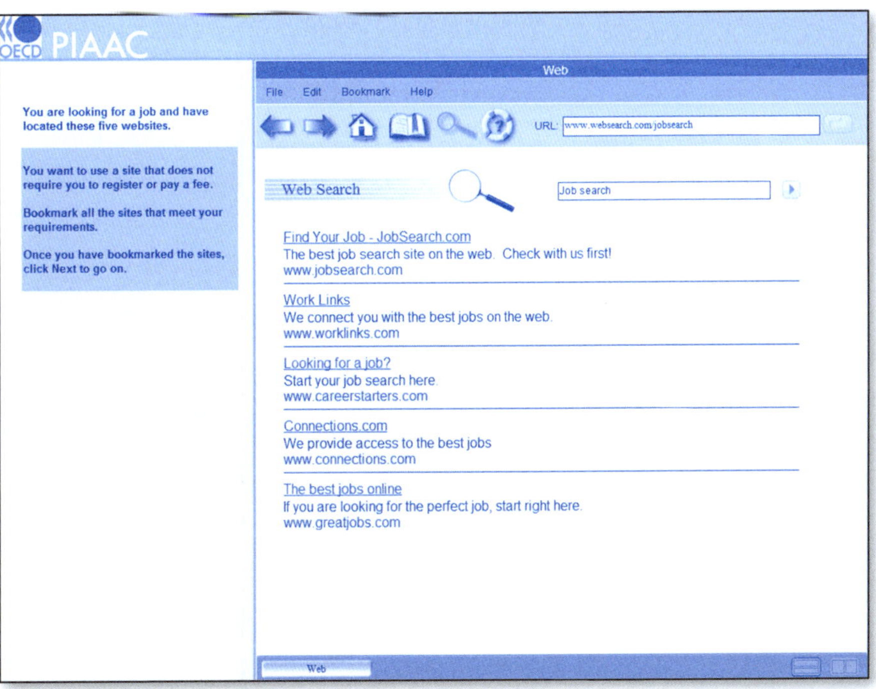

As can be seen, this item requires that respondents work within a simulated web environment that includes tools and functionality similar to those found in real-life applications. Users are able to:

- Click on links on both the results page and associated web pages;
- Navigate using the back and forward arrows or the Home icon; and
- Bookmark web pages and view or change those bookmarks.

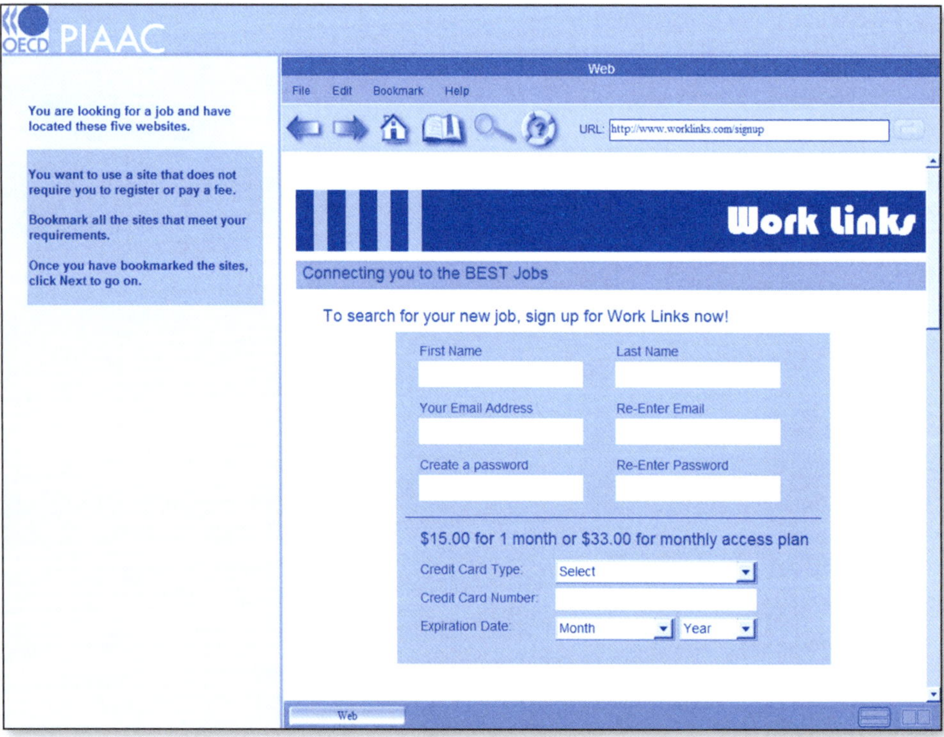

In order to perform this task correctly, respondents may have to search through several pages on a website. One of the features of PIAAC is that the process and paths by which a respondent responds to the tasks is captured. For example, one of the websites, presented below, does not meet the criteria of not requiring registration or the payment of a fee, but the relevant information is not on the opening page. If a respondent bookmarks this site without clicking on the "Learn More" link to view the relevant information (see the website on the following page), this response may be interpreted in a different way than if the relevant page had been viewed. The breadth of information, combined with frameworks that specify behaviours of interest, allow us to learn more about what adults know and can do relative to the construct of problem solving.

The relevant information is located on the form that indicates that users must sign up (register) and pay a fee.

Sample Item 2

In this item of level 2 difficulty, respondents select a set of files to download onto a portable music player. The files must meet specified criteria in terms of genre (jazz and rock) and not exceed the capacity of the device (maximum of 20 MB).

The software includes an automatic summing functionality ("Total Size Selected") that facilitates the task by updating the total file size as files are selected or de-selected. Respondents must monitor progress as they select files, checking against the specified criteria to know when they have satisfied the constraints presented in the problem.

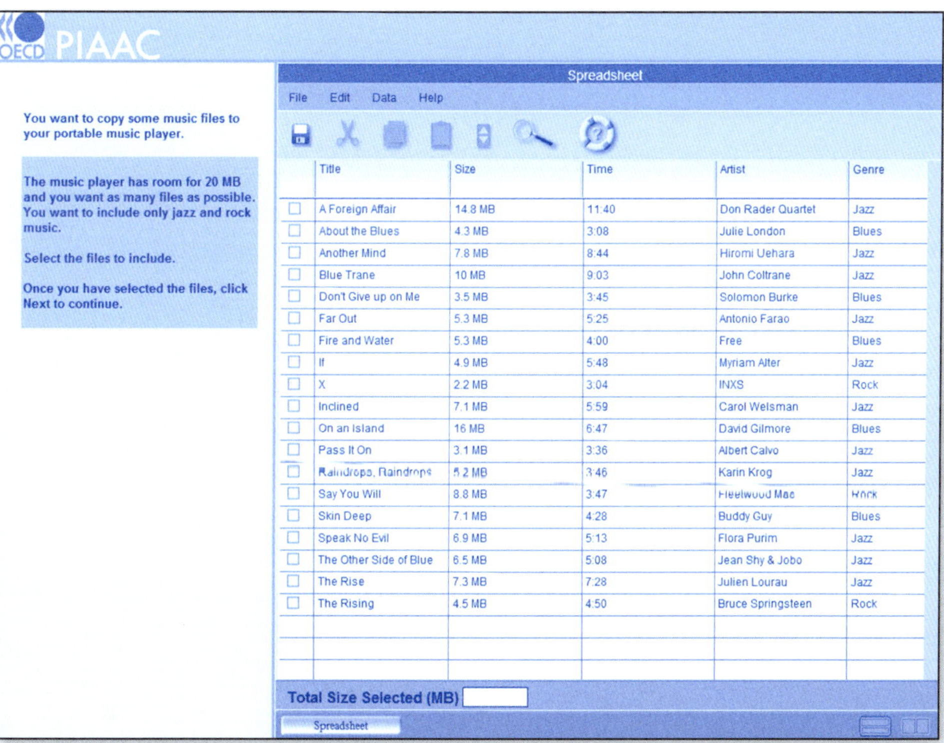

	Title	Size	Time	Artist	Genre
☐	A Foreign Affair	14.8 MB	11:40	Don Rader Quartet	Jazz
☐	About the Blues	4.3 MB	3:08	Julie London	Blues
☐	Another Mind	7.8 MB	8:44	Hiromi Uehara	Jazz
☐	Blue Trane	10 MB	9:03	John Coltrane	Jazz
☐	Don't Give up on Me	3.5 MB	3:45	Solomon Burke	Blues
☐	Far Out	5.3 MB	5:25	Antonio Farao	Jazz
☐	Fire and Water	5.3 MB	4:00	Free	Blues
☐	If	4.9 MB	5:48	Myriam Alter	Jazz
☐	X	2.2 MB	3:04	INXS	Rock
☐	Inclined	7.1 MB	5:59	Carol Welsman	Jazz
☐	On an Island	16 MB	6:47	David Gilmore	Blues
☐	Pass It On	3.1 MB	3:36	Albert Calvo	Jazz
☐	Raindrops, Raindrops	5.2 MB	3:46	Karin Krog	Jazz
☐	Say You Will	8.8 MB	3:47	Fleetwood Mac	Rock
☐	Skin Deep	7.1 MB	4:28	Buddy Guy	Blues
☐	Speak No Evil	6.9 MB	5:13	Flora Purim	Jazz
☐	The Other Side of Blue	6.5 MB	5:08	Jean Shy & Jobo	Jazz
☐	The Rise	7.3 MB	7:28	Julien Lourau	Jazz
☐	The Rising	4.5 MB	4:50	Bruce Springsteen	Rock

It is also possible to sort the spreadsheet by file size and/or genre, a strategy that can improve task efficiency. The connection between the use of resources in a technology-rich environment and resulting efficiencies for solving problems is emphasised in the framework and therefore included across items in the assessment.

References

Lennon, M., et al. (2003), *Feasibility Study for the PISA ICT Literacy Assessment,* Educational Testing Services, Princeton, New Jersey.

Annex A
Members of the Subject Matter Expert Groups

PIAAC Literacy Expert Group

Stan Jones (Chair), Canada
Egil Gabrielsen, Center for Reading Research, University of Stavanger, Norway
Jan Hagston, Australia
Pirjo Linnakylä, University of Jyväskylä, Finland
Hakima Megherbi, University of Paris, France
John Sabatini, Educational Testing Service, United States of America
Monika Tröster, German Institute for Adult Education, Germany
Eduardo Vidal-Abarca, Department of Psychology, University of Valencia, Spain

PIAAC Numeracy Expert Group

Iddo Gal (Chair), University of Haifa, Israel
Silvia Alatorre, National Pedagogical University, Mexico
Sean Close, St. Patrick's College, Ireland
Jeff Evans, Middlesex University, United Kingdom
Lene Johansen, Aalborg University, Denmark
Terry Maguire, Institute of Technology Tallaght-Dublin, Ireland
Myrna Manly, United States of America
Dave Tout, Australian Council for Educational Research, Australia

PIAAC Problem Solving in Technology-Rich Environments Expert Group

Jean-François Rouet (Chair), CNRS and University of Poitiers, France
Mirelle Bétrancourt, University of Geneva, Switzerland
M. Anne Britt, Northern Illinois University, United States of America
Dr. Rainer Bromme, University of Muenster, Germany
Arthur C. Graesser, University of Memphis, United States of America
Jonna M. Kulikowich, Pennsylvania State University, United States of America
Donald J. Leu, University of Connecticut, United States of America
Naoki Ueno, Musashi Institute of Technology, Japan
Herre van Oostendorp, Utrecht University, Netherlands

PIAAC Reading Components Expert Group

John P. Sabatini, Educational Testing Service, United States of America
Kelly M. Bruce, Educational Testing Service, United States of America

ORGANISATION FOR ECONOMIC CO-OPERATION AND DEVELOPMENT

The OECD is a unique forum where governments work together to address the economic, social and environmental challenges of globalisation. The OECD is also at the forefront of efforts to understand and to help governments respond to new developments and concerns, such as corporate governance, the information economy and the challenges of an ageing population. The Organisation provides a setting where governments can compare policy experiences, seek answers to common problems, identify good practice and work to co-ordinate domestic and international policies.

The OECD member countries are: Australia, Austria, Belgium, Canada, Chile, the Czech Republic, Denmark, Estonia, Finland, France, Germany, Greece, Hungary, Iceland, Ireland, Israel, Italy, Japan, Korea, Luxembourg, Mexico, the Netherlands, New Zealand, Norway, Poland, Portugal, the Slovak Republic, Slovenia, Spain, Sweden, Switzerland, Turkey, the United Kingdom and the United States. The European Commission takes part in the work of the OECD.

OECD Publishing disseminates widely the results of the Organisation's statistics gathering and research on economic, social and environmental issues, as well as the conventions, guidelines and standards agreed by its members.

OECD PUBLISHING, 2, rue André-Pascal, 75775 PARIS CEDEX 16
(87 2012 03 1 P) ISBN 978-92-64-12880-4 – No. 59751 2012-05